TOWARD WHAT JUSTICE?

Toward What Justice? brings together compelling ideas from a wide range of intellectual traditions in education to discuss corresponding and sometimes competing definitions of justice. Leading scholars articulate new ideas and challenge entrenched views of what justice means when considered from the perspectives of diverse communities. Their chapters, written boldly and pressing directly into the difficult and even strained questions of justice, reflect on the contingencies and incongruences at work when considering what justice wants and requires. At its heart, *Toward What Justice?* is a book about justice projects, and the incommensurable investments that social justice projects can make. It is a must-have volume for scholars and students working at the intersection of education and Indigenous studies, critical disability studies, climate change research, queer studies, and more.

Eve Tuck is Associate Professor of Critical Race and Indigenous Studies at the Ontario Institute for Studies in Education (OISE), University of Toronto.

K. Wayne Yang is Associate Professor in Ethnic Studies at the University of California, San Diego.

TOWARD WHAT JUSTICE?

Describing Diverse Dreams of Justice in Education

Edited by Eve Tuck and K. Wayne Yang

Routledge
Taylor & Francis Group

NEW YORK AND LONDON

First published 2018
by Routledge
711 Third Avenue, New York, NY 10017

and by Routledge
2 Park Square, Milton Park, Abingdon, Oxon, OX14 4RN

Routledge is an imprint of the Taylor & Francis Group, an informa business

© 2018 Taylor & Francis

Library of Congress Cataloging-in-Publication Data
Names: Tuck, Eve, editor. | Yang, K. Wayne, editor.
Title: Toward what justice? : describing diverse dreams of justice in
education / edited by Eve Tuck and K. Wayne Yang.
Description: New York, NY : Routledge, 2018. | Includes bibliographical
references and index.
Identifiers: LCCN 2017047016 | ISBN 9781138205710 (hbk : alk. paper) |
ISBN 9781351240932 (ebk)
Subjects: LCSH: Educational equalization. | Social justice. |
Education—Aims and objectives.
Classification: LCC LC213 .T7 2018 | DDC 379.2/6—dc23
LC record available at https://lccn.loc.gov/2017047016

ISBN: 978-1-138-20572-7 (hbk)
ISBN: 978-1-138-20571-0 (pbk)
ISBN: 978-1-351-24093-2 (ebk)

Typeset in Bembo
by Out of House Publishing

CONTENTS

ACKNOWLEDGEMENTS

We rose with the sun to make our acknowledgements, to give our most heartfelt thanks.

This book marks the tenth year of our collaboration, which has spanned conference organizing, co-authoring, co-editing—books, guest-edited special issues, a book series with Routledge called *Indigenous and Decolonizing Studies in Education*, and a journal, *Critical Ethnic Studies*. Together we also founded the Land Relationships Super Collective, which bodes the future entanglements of our work. To our communities and collaborators on all of these activities, these futures, we are grateful; we are awed.

This book began as a presidential panel called Toward What Justice? Describing Diverse Dreams of Justice in Education, presented at the 2015 Annual Meeting of the American Educational Research Association.[1] Our co-panelists included Leigh Patel, Nirmala Erevelles, Michael Dumas, Jen Jack Gieseking, and the discussant was Kris Gutierrez.

The panel itself was inspired by 2015 AERA President Joyce King's annual meeting theme, *Toward Justice: Culture, Language, and Heritage in Education Research and Praxis*. The title of the theme borrows from the observation by Dr. Martin Luther King, Jr., that the "arc of the moral universe is long, but it bends toward justice." Dr. Martin Luther King, Jr. was paraphrasing from a speech by 19th-century minister Theodore Parker, arguing for the abolition of slavery. We remain thankful for the space that Joyce King's annual theme created in the association, and for the interventions made possible through this call.

Many others have contributed to this book, often by responding across many modes of communication. We are constantly learning from Megan Bang's brilliant collaborative research on environmental justice and the need to attend to Indigenous knowledges, design, and leadership in addressing climate change. Bang's work has engaged and theorized different understandings of justice for many years. We cannot thank Susan Blight without laughing at ourselves—so, as a small inside joke, we thank her for helping us in ways that Google Translate never could. To Chani Nicholas, we express thanks for calling forth the complexities of our complicities and resistances to colonialism, as part of our historical preparation for this moment: *We are here for this... We are made for this.*[2]

Christi Belcourt and the Onaman Collective keep our focus on what is already underway, what has already gained momentum across lands and waters. By allowing us to revise her last keynote into the penultimate chapter of this volume, she brings this hopeful, relentless message to you: the revolution has already begun. Belcourt's soul-nourishing artwork is on the cover of this volume, which is a great honor. The Onaman Collective is working to establish *Nimkii Aazhibikoong*, a site for land- and arts-based language and life learning.[3] Some of the proceeds from this book will be directed to the Onaman Collective and Nimkii Aazhibikoong.

Our colleague Antonio Martinez is exactly whom we were holding in our hearts as we completed this volume; we care about what he would have thought of it.

Many other colleagues and students have been in our thoughts as we made this book. We deeply respect the teachers, organizers, artists, and students who have fought for justice in the streets, on the page, on the bricks, through campaigns, punches, poetry, murals, and syllabi. The explicitness of hatred that is being expressed by elected leaders and those who elected them is an assault, though that hatred has always been coursing through settler colonial societies. Often this hatred is so commonplace that no one bothers to keep it beneath the surface: this is the part of the arc we are in now, and it has been long.

We love, love working with Catherine Bernard, and appreciate all of the ways in which our writing and thinking blossom with her guidance. Deanna DelVecchio, a PhD candidate at the Ontario Institute for Studies in Education, University of Toronto, has been a radiant and fastidious contributor to this volume through managing much of the correspondence, chapters, editing, and even co-authoring the final chapter. This volume has been changed for the better because of her astute attention.

Our families are places—for our celebrations, our grief, our dashed expectations—that hold us as we do all of this holding. Broken hearts are mended there, fears made safe there. To our families who remind us of the balancing act of working and living, of desolation and joy, and do so much for the plus side of living and joy, we offer our everlasting gramercy.

Eve Tuck and K. Wayne Yang

Notes

1 www.aera.net/Events-Meetings/Annual-Meeting/Previous-Annual-Meetings/2015-Annual-Meeting/2015-Annual-Meeting-Webcasts/Toward-What-Justice-Describing-Diverse-Dreams-of-Justice-in-Education
2 http://chaninicholas.com/2016/10/honoring-our-ancestors-sundays-new-moon-in-scorpio/
3 http://onamancollective.com/research/

INTRODUCTION

Born Under the Rising Sign of Social Justice

Eve Tuck and K. Wayne Yang

If you are like us, the impulse to dream and work toward justice may feel like it was part of your being since before your birth. The pull toward working for justice can feel transhistorical, like you heard it whispered by ancestors or felt it transmitted back to you from a future-in-waiting. It may feel immensely strong and encompassing, like gravity, both planetary and personal, all at once. It may have shaped your education in and out of schooling, your day jobs and your night shifts, your relationships, your breakups, your sense of home and of movement. This pulse for justice may feel like a rising constellation that presides over your predispositions and the choices which, together, add up to your destiny.

It is to you, to all of us, who were born under the rising sign of social justice, that we dedicate this book.

We are not sure when this sign first broke over the horizon. It rises repeatedly, blazes long, and returns quickly after setting. The sign moves in elliptical cycles over this sky, dwelling longer than a year, disappearing and returning with a hyperbolic quickness. It marks seasons that stretch over years, like the drawn-out winter that threatens to arrive. Social justice is an epoch, and we are living in it. Thus, several generations have been born under this sign. Even at its apogee—its point which is farthest away from us—the sign of social justice has its influence.

Like people born under any rising sign, the place and time of your birth matters. Those differences provide the multiple viewpoints from which various justice projects are imagined and carried out. No two people of the same sign are identical in personality or in politics. Even so, there is often a mutual recognition by people of the same sign. This book acknowledges the diverse dreaming that has happened under this rising sign, and also acknowledges that those dreams are not so far apart, even while they may be incommensurable in their goals. We have written before (Tuck & Yang, 2012) about an ethic of incommensurability as an alternate mode of holding and imagining solidarity. Rather than the goal of political unity with commonly shared objectives, an ethic of incommensurability acknowledges that we can collaborate for a time together even while anticipating that our pathways toward enacting liberation will diverge. Incommensurability means that we cannot judge each other's justice projects by the same standard, but we can come to understand the gap between our viewpoints, and thus work together in contingent collaboration.

That said, incommensurability does not necessarily mean separations of great distance. Incommensurability can be quite close, as close as two people holding hands under the same sign. An ethic of incommensurability is apprehending the small inner angle made between those two beings and the sign above. A separation as wide as the earth is a small inner angle with respect to the stars above.

The sign of social justice has influenced the dreaming of those born under it; this part of it we feel most sure about. There is truth in Martin Carter's poetry, that we "do not sleep to dream, but dream to change the world."

To be together in this world, working and living under this sign, involves a mutual acknowledgement, even as our terms fall apart in the space between us. In this book, and this introduction, there are vexed terms all over the place (justice itself included). We are sorting between many goals which could have animated this discussion, including goals of complete and total coherence (impossible) and goals of complete clarity and consistency (boring). We use the words we can, even when they disappoint or obscure. Sometimes, it is good just to say, "I feel what you are trying to say with those words and it does not matter that I use those words with a different meaning." Again, it is the inner angle made between us.

Inner Angles Made between Us

Eve's first publications described a way to imagine the relationship between varying approaches to making social change by thinking about inner angles. Inner angles is a spatial way of thinking about how theories of change—even those which are embedded in constructs of justice which are incommensurable with others—are related to other theories of change (Tuck, 2009; Tuck & Fine, 2007). When things are contradistinctive from each other they might be mapped as two poles on a spectrum, two dots with a line between them. Cardinal directions mapped as two perpendicular lines with N, S, E & W also can give the impression of four poles with lines in between them. If we think of theories of change as poles, with lines between them (even if these lines are a spectrum of gradation between those theories of change), we can get a false impression that moving between theories of change requires great effort or journeying. Paying attention only to the polarity of theories of change, the exterior contours of their shape and definition, can be misleading in terms of thinking about how theories of change can be in relation to each other. Instead, we might consider the inner angles created in mapping these poles, the sharp corners, the wide wedges which meet on the inside. If we consider those inner angles for their feature of the way that an angle does not have a length, then we can be concerned not with the distance between ideas, but the small shifts that can cross them. For readers who have ever held a young one on their laps or on a hip, consider the weight of the baby, how the weight and pressure grows more intense with passing time. Then, consider the physical sensation of moving that young one to the other hip, or off the lap, or to another knee. New vantage points, new movements, new somatic possibilities are made through that small shift. This is the simple idea at the center of the metaphor of an inner angle.

In wayfinding, being a few degrees off and proceeding for a long time in the miscalculated direction can result in being miles and miles away from the intended destination. The small shifts at the outset are the stuff of inner angles. When the angles are close, small shifts might cross what will otherwise become insurmountable divides.

Inner angles—small shifts of weight as in moving a baby from one hip to another, small shifts which can be made and will impact how far apart from another we find ourselves—are a stark contrast to the prominent symbology of state justice that is so pervasive: the scales held by "Lady Justice." These are symbols of justice which hold influence throughout Western colonial geopolitical spaces. Scales of Justice are usually depicted as two shallow dishes held by chains on a fulcrum, or balance. The scales are usually golden or made of stone, and they are held by a woman draped in something referencing more ancient Greek garb. She is supposed to be Dike, the daughter of Zeus and Themis, and an arbiter of rules. She always wears a blindfold, to convey the ways that justice is "blind" or "objective." Of course, it would be much more interesting to think of the ways that justice is blindfolded, but instead, blindness is used as a vacated ableist metaphor in this instance, as is often the case.

This, the major symbolic communicator for what constitutes state justice, is hard to take seriously. These scales represent another kind of project: a worldview that state justice is a balance of competing interests, that takes for its strategy an arbitrator with a supremacist power of law, with the motive of maintaining order, combined with practices of appealing to state power. In reality, state justice does not operate this way; it has cages and swords but no scales. State justice is not in balance; it is not in scale. The apparatuses of justice do not correspond to the scales of individuals, of communities, of nations that they operate on. We wish we had a more fitting symbol for justice to offer you. Maybe all we can offer is the notion of justice with a rising sign, creating an inner angle with the horizon, and those people and non-human persons on the earth pointing their faces toward it.

A Warm Ambivalence about the Term "Social Justice"

Perhaps because it is a term not always treated with respect in the academy, "social justice" is used frequently but rarely defined. Social justice is now commonly associated with many aspects of fields of education, reflected in titles of conferences, book series, journals, and academic departments. At the same time, at least one major educational research association and its journals maintain distance from the term, citing the need to remain objective or neutral in order to remain inclusive of all potential members and readers. We have a lot of admiration, affection, and kinship with people who use social justice to define their work, who were born under the rising sign of justice. In prior writings, we have looked closely at terms, wondering what others mean by them, what we mean by them, and the work those terms can and cannot do. We did this with "resistance" (Tuck & Yang, 2014), with "identity" (Tuck & Yang, 2017), and we have done this elsewhere with the word "justice" (Tuck & Yang, 2016). We are trying very hard to not make this our thing, that we take a word that means a great deal to conversations in the field of education that have otherwise been shut down, and then write into it so heavily that the term dematerializes. While this type of analysis has its uses, we are trying to avoid dematerializing the term "justice," for now. We do not want to turn justice into a fugitive subject which cannot be known and fully described. It is not mysterious.

"Social justice" is a term used to describe the organizations, schools, programs, departments, and institutes that have employed us, and that we have founded. It is a term that has been associated with a great deal of our professional labor over the years. We understand the irony of the appropriation of this term, and the simultaneous acknowledgement and domestication of our work. Over the past several years that we have been heavily engaged with social justice as a term and as a category of work in the academic field, we have been struck by the reasoning of those who have refused to use that term in their work (Simpson, 2016; Dumas, this volume; Walcott, this volume). These authors discard the term for its lack of specificity, for its deferrals, for its investments in the state, for its distractions. We continue to learn from the abdications of the term by our friends, teachers, and colleagues.

Here, we want to talk about "social justice" as words that work as a signal in the field of education, but also in other fields such as law, and social science fields. In the interdisciplinary field of education, the term "social justice" works to set certain approaches and aims apart from positivist approaches. Thus, for those of us in education who reject positivist and developmental paradigms, social justice has been a way to signal to ourselves and to one another this epistemological and political difference. Social justice is a way to mark a distinction from the origins and habits of almost all disciplines which emerged in the 19th and 20th centuries and are rooted in colonialism and white supremacy. Social justice education is a way to refer to all research and practice within the domains of education which are a departure from behavioral or cognitive or developmental approaches. This is, of course, not to say that individuals who locate their work in these disciplines do not care about improving the lives of everyday people, but that social justice education has been a way for those outside of those disciplines to still find a home in education and schools of education. Social justice education is a self-conscious exception to the otherwise teleological imperatives of what has, up until now, typified the field(s) of education.

In this way, social justice education has served the role of the "other" box on surveys—think of how race or language might appear on a survey—a catchall term for those who find themselves outside of the sanctioned intellectual traditions of education. Still, the need for a term that serves the function of an "other" box is still abundantly apparent because much of what gets researched and published within the field of education is actually research that pathologizes communities, youth, children, and families. So much of what gets circulated is still squawking about getting communities, youth, children, and families caught up with white and middle-class people, as Leigh Patel critiques in Chapter 6. People who use social justice as a signal for what their work engages with understand that inequities are produced, inequities are structured, and that things have got to change in order to achieve different educational outcomes. Social justice education is a *choice away* from pathology and linearity.

Because it is such an important choice away, because it represents such a pertinent epistemological and methodological departure from other commonplace practices in the field, many groups of students and faculties in universities have attempted to institutionalize social justice education. However, institutionalizing social justice education has its deep contradictions. These reasons are expounded throughout the book, and openly addressed in Chapter 5 by Rinaldo Walcott and in Chapter 3 by Sandy Grande. As a whole, this book is agnostic about the institutionalization of social justice education into departments or programs. Aspects of branding, innovation, and credentialism come into play, as is true with the institutionalization of any field or discipline that has emerged to counter mainstream academic practices and theories. We do not say that all education programs should be called social justice programs. Rather, we say that social justice is the ghost in the machine of the educational apparatus. It is the only part that makes any part of the field of education matter.

With or without formally institutionalizing social justice education, it is not a countercultural movement within the broader field of education. Thus, this book is not about some boutique aspect of the field of education, some little meandering down a curious alley. This is not a conversation at the margins of a field. Social justice education—whether or not we continue to use those words to define it—is the crux of the future of our field. Social justice is not the other of the field of education, it *is* the field. There is no future of the field of education without the contributions of people who are doing their work under the rising sign of social justice. There is no legitimacy to the field of education if it cannot meaningfully attend to social contexts, historical and contemporary structures of settler colonialism, white supremacy, and antiblackness. Social justice is not the catchall; it is the all.

A Book about Justice Projects

Much is presumed about what is meant by social justice in education, but when considered from the perspectives of diverse communities and their concerns, social justice takes on varying and sometimes contradictory meanings. As a catchall term, social justice does a lot to try to contain multiple perspectives and futurities. Social justice for one group may mean greater integration and mobility within the dominant society, whereas that definition for another group may be regarded as futile. The aspirational goal of one project may be regarded as foreclosure of another project. Indeed, notions of justice may actually compete in some circumstances.

This is a book about justice projects and the competing investments that social justice projects can make. This far in, we have to point out again that many of the words in the previous line are imperfect: *competing, investments, projects.* We say this anyway, knowing that our words are reaching, straining to convey something about how what we believe about how justice and injustice materializes, matters.

"Competing" isn't exactly the word—indeed, for reasons we described above, we prefer the word "incommensurable" to competing. But just for a moment, we stay with the way in which "competing" reveals how some projects undermine others, quash others, make other projects seem ridiculous or impossible. As many of the authors in this book will detail, liberal and multicultural renderings of the relationships between social justice projects have generated an almost list-based approach. This approach is at work when people are writing a shared statement and listing either all of the communities, all of the experiences of oppression, or all of the social structures that are at the center of their attention or practice. People sometimes refer to this as attending to "the isms," which we suspect no one likes doing, as it is an odd mixture of being inclusive (liberal) and actually attending to difference (radical). It shows how the foundation of this kind of thinking is inclusion by list making, by making objects appear on a list of what matters. Then, because the lists get long when they are at their best, there are broader terms or acronyms created to refer to the list. The list is a product of liberal multicultural thinking, but there aren't sufficient alternatives. The list will have to do for now. What we want to raise about the list, however, is the possibility that experiences and projects in a given list may not cohabitate; they may even be antagonistic. Projects attending to Indigenous rematriation of land and life cannot be absorbed into projects which do not interrogate and forgo concepts of property. Projects attending to Black liberation and abolition cannot be absorbed into projects which do not interrogate and forgo concepts of the human. These are just two examples which are discussed at length throughout this book.

"Investments" is also a miserable word, but it, too, does some work in describing what this book is trying to do. All the synonyms of investment carry the scent of capitalism, and we are not exactly trying to escape the connotations of money and wealth that come with it. By investment, we are talking about how using a term or concept makes it somehow more prominent and more likely to be used by someone else. Like a path in tall grasses, choosing one path instead of others, over time, will make that path more obvious. Paths become deep-set grooves and, over time, can appear to be the only option. Eve's brother teases her for listening to the playlist on her iPod® that has been automatically created out of the top 25 songs she listens to most frequently. Each time she listens to that playlist, she is cementing that those are the top 25 songs, and making it less likely that other songs can ever break into the top 25. This is the way it works with regard to the investments that various social justice projects make. Over time, with repetition of use, other possibilities become less possible. Investments make some paths possible, and others untraceable.

We use the word "projects" instead of other options, such as framework, episte-mology or axiology, because "projects" connotes the specificity of work, of praxis. Imagine that we visit one another, in a place, in a community, in the midst of an endeavor, in a historical moment, and we respectfully ask ourselves, "What is the project here?" In asking this question, we are trying to understand: what is at work in all of this work? What does this work care about? What animates and compels this work? What does this work believe about itself and others? For this reason, in this usage of project we do not mean it as a discrete unit of human time and labor, such as a research project, class project, or youth project. We use project as a way to refer to worldview combined with strategy combined with motive combined with practices and habits.

It is exciting that Stuart Hall's work is finding new readers through volumes published in a series by Duke University Press, edited by Catherine Hall and Bill Schwarz. Hall's works are immensely relevant to conversations in social justice education, critical ethnic studies, or any group of people working on ideas at the threshold of institutionalization. Our colleague Rinaldo Walcott has always been a close reader of Hall's work, and when we noticed how Walcott is deploying the term "projects" in Chapter 5 in this volume, we put the question about the legacy of the term to him. Walcott directed us to Hall's classic essay, "Cultural Studies and its Theoretical Legacies" (1992). Here, Hall uses the word "project," as in the project of cultural studies, without necessarily defining it—Hall teaches the use of the word in context, by using it. It is clear that a project, for Hall, is referring to an intervention, to a practice as politics. Projects like cultural studies hold "theoretical and political questions in an ever irresolvable but permanent tension" (p. 288). Responding to a prompt to say more about that permanent tension, Hall observes:

> I think that just as we have to understand politics as a language we have to understand politics as living with the tension. The notion of a political prac-tice where criticism is postponed until the day after the barricades precisely defines the politics which I always refused. And if you don't go that way you go into politics of contention, of continuous argument, of continuous debate. Because what is at stake really matters.

Finally, then, the question of the manner in which our tensions are worked through matters a great deal. I don't want to prescribe but I want to draw your attention to the problem of courtesy, of living with a tension that matters without eating each other. Because there is a kind of competitive way in which intellectuals live with their tensions in which they can only do so by climbing on the backs of those people whose positions they're trying to contest. We have a great deal to learn about respecting the positions being advanced while contesting them because something important is at stake. I don't think we're very good at that. We have a lot to learn about the manners of a genuinely dialogically critical engagement.

(Hall, 1992, p. 290)

Because of Hall's influence on our teachers, our colleagues, and our past and future works, when we refer to projects here and elsewhere, we mean serious work at the nexus of staunch tensions, carried out with genuine commitment to critical engagement. We mean to do it without eating each other. We mean to do it as a way of life.

Two Compelling Justice Projects: Abolition and Decolonization

There are social justice projects which we find compelling, which move us, which call our names; and there are those that flatten us. We tend to refuse the many projects with theories of change that rely upon the benevolence of the state or of the dominant in society.

We refuse:

- Justice projects which require us to prove humanity or worth
- Justice projects which require us to frontload a lot of learning or consciousness-raising
- Justice projects which require us to appeal to the people who abuse us
- Justice projects which require us to gather an audience of white settlers who are presumed to have agency
- Justice projects that presume compromise as the main avenue for achieving solidarity

Having made this list, we understand that there are social justice projects which may be quite complicit in any or all of the above, and that we may have benefited from them. We are not presenting this list as dogma. We feel the words of Frances S. Lee (2017) that if there is a church of social justice, then "excommunicate me" from it. Rather, we are clarifying the whys and why nots of our own participation. We are tracing the arcs of our inner angles.

The projects that do call our names these days are on abolition and decolonization. Abolition is a movement to end slavery, to abolish institutions of unfreedom, a movement that has necessarily and repeatedly unsettled the foundations of modern capital (Bassichis, Lee, & Spade, 2011; Davis, 2011; Gilmore, 2007; Meiners, 2011). Abolition shook the plantation economies of the Americas and the Caribbean, and their legal and moral apparatuses that ensured enslavement of Indigenous African and American peoples. Abolition is shaking the antiblack institutions that underwrite whiteness as property (Harris, 1993), that sanction murder, captivity, torture, and disposal: namely, the prison industrial complex.

Decolonization is the rematriation of Indigenous land and life. Decolonization, similar to abolition, unsettles the ways that land has become alienable into property; that animals, plants, water, air and earth have become alienable into "natural resources" to be turned into profit; that occupiers and their governments can come to have sovereignty over Indigenous people and places. Decolonization as an imperative has made and unmade nation-states, unmade and remade rights to land, unmade and remade the individual or corporate entities that are understood to have legal custody over peoples and places.

There are, admittedly, some tensions between how scholars in Black studies and scholars in Indigenous studies have interpreted these projects, and especially how they have interpreted projects criss-crossing these disciplinary boundaries. We are exasperated with some of the practices of using Black people as a foil, or counterpoint, to arguments in Indigenous studies, and of using Indigenous people as the contrast for arguments made in Black studies (see also Latty, Scribe, Peters & Morgan, 2016; Palacios, 2016). We are interested in what Eve's colleague Miglena Todorova teaches in her courses as the difference between a relational analysis and a comparative analysis, which is the focus of this book (see also Volume 1, Issue 2 of *Critical Ethnic Studies*, on Racial Comparativism Reconsidered, edited by Danika Medak-Saltzman and Antonio T. Tiongson, Jr.). Thus, we are compelled by the ways in which Indigenous and Black scholarship might be engaged together to contest the violence and legitimacy of the nation-state and its apparatuses, and to refuse routes to justice which require us to appeal for our humanity. Consider these words, from Dionne Brand, speaking at Barnard College, Colombia University, in April 2017:

> In our case, I believe that we live in a state of tyranny. And to ask a tyranny to dismantle itself, to claim, to ask for, to invoke justice is to present our bodies already consigned in that tyranny to the status of nonbeing, to ask the state to bring us into being. And that is impossible and it won't. That state is anathema to us, and so I do not write toward anything called justice, but against tyranny, and toward liberation.
>
> *(Brand, 2017)*

Leanne Simpson makes a similar observation, writing, "I am not particularly interested in holding states accountable because the structure, history and nature of states is exploitative in nature" (2016, p. 31). Both abolition and decolonization object to the configuration of the nation-state in its specificity (the United States,

Canada, Israel, New Zealand, South Africa, Australia, and so on), and its generaliz-ability. Such a social order, and its violences, cannot be made just; cannot be made good.

Though the need for these projects cannot be disputed, the frequent response by sympathetic liberals and even people committed to radical social change is that abolition is unimaginable and that decolonization is philosophical but not practical. This is the observation that Dan Berger, Mariame Kaba, and David Stein make in an article in *Jacobin Magazine* titled "What Abolitionists Do" (2017). Linking abolition to fights against chattel slavery, private property, and the prison indus-trial complex, the authors note that abolition is always discarded as utopian, not practical, even by those who describe themselves as working for social change. Instead, Berger, Kaba, and Stein observe that abolition is a "lodestar and practical necessity" (2017, n.p.). Describing how abolition is both a naming of a goal and navigating the divide between current state violence and the eradication of state/ violence, the authors share the variety of activities which have come to be part of abolition projects. The gains of these activities are their own proof of the need and possibility for abolition. Likewise, there are many practical efforts to rematriate Indigenous land and life, from restoring Indigenous foodways, to turning land out of the property system, to restoring languages.

When people automatically dismiss the possibilities for abolition and decolo-nization, they rarely acknowledge how this reaction is entrenched in competing projects. Indeed, because abolition and decolonization are lodestars—stars which are used to guide our course—*and* practical, abolition and decolonization are not projects to be deferred for the next generation. They are happening next; they are happening now. Abolition and decolonization are rupturing into the mainstream with movements for Black life and defenders of Indigenous lands and waters, as much as people wish to contain #BlackLivesMatter to the plan of reducing dis-crimination in policing or Idle No More or #NoDAPL to the goals of environ-mentalism. Abolition and decolonization have always been happening, since the advent of a Western imperial worldview equated with modernity that took hold around 1492. Alternative societies, and the dismantling of slavery and its institu-tions, have been constant projects comprising serious work at the site of staunch tensions.

These projects are happening now.

Neither abolition nor decolonization are philosophies. They are practical routes. Abolition and decolonization are practices. The people engaged in them are among the most pragmatic on earth—they understand that these have to be happening now, because of the consequences of living beyond the capacity of the earth to heal itself without destroying all people. As Christi Belcourt makes plain in Chapter 7, the revolution has already begun.

In our own writing on decolonization and our reading of works on abolition, we emphasize that neither abolition nor decolonization are endpoints. They are impera-tives. They are not a promised land or future. They are exactly what drive our work and attention. Yet, this is where it matters to consider how there is not a one-to-one relationship between injustice and justice. There is not a direct trajectory from the harm to the justice. Said another way, we should not think that slavery is what drives our demands for abolition. We should not think that colonization is what drives our demands for decolonization. Again, we can pursue these imperatives without being locked into a false linearity between cause and effect. Decolonization is not the effect of the cause called colonization. Decolonization defies ongoing colonization.

The title of this volume, *Toward What Justice?* asks several questions. It questions the forms of justice that we think we want. What justice? It questions the compass points of our work, the directions we are taking that we sometimes mistake as endpoints. Toward what? Justice? To think of justice as an imperative, rather than as an end, might help us put our own justice projects in relation to others. Our theorizing is enhanced when we understand how projects are fulfilling an imperative, answering a calling inspired by the rising sign of social justice.

To this end, we have playfully considered how we might create a notation for the "toward" of justice. This playfulness of thought is what generated our opening motif of being born under the rising sign of justice. How might we indicate what is rising in our justice projects? One idea is an arrow, a toward, which marks what the project is aiming toward. The "what toward" of justice. Might the toward become a rising? $\rightarrow$ is a notational device that conveys how we won't be satisfied with social justice, but always a social justice $\rightarrow$ [what]. The arrow is a reminder of the demands of justice projects. The arrow is an indicator of intention, of futurity.

Abolition $\rightarrow$ Black life   Decolonization $\rightarrow$ Indigenous futures

In this notation, the arrows do not mean that Black life is not already happening or that Indigenous futures are not already happening. In some ways, Black life is what demands abolition. Indigenous futures demand decolonization, rather than abolition births Black life or decolonization births Indigenous futures.

Chapters Waiting for You

We encourage readers to read each chapter for its projects; to use the project as the unit of analysis. Then, you might consider the inner angles formed between projects described and your own projects. To attend to the inner angles, you could shift a step or a seat to the side, and notice what movements, routes, and vantages are made possible. Reading in this way can produce a more intimate reading; one that is less likely to be overshadowed by a project that is claiming much light. This is the work of reading for a relational analysis, rather than a comparative analysis.

Our book opens with prison abolition. Crystal Laura's "Against Prisons and the Pipeline to Them" is public pedagogy in the form of a written essay. It not only provides a clear argument for abolition, it also does the work of provoking the imagination necessary for the will to fight for abolition and its practices. It is an essay capable of engaging many different kinds of readers: prison abolitionists looking for an affirming essay to share; people who might already sympathize with but not understand abolition; and people who cannot imagine abolition. Generous with voice and with her experiences, Laura presents the Freedom Square, an encampment and vibrant community space erected opposite the notorious Chicago police's Homan Square, a "black site" where thousands of people disappear into police custody. Chicago Freedom Square is an example of the practice of abolition—the practices, relations, and mutual accountability that Black communities can and do create as alternatives to the violating forms of justice promised by the police. Laura also shares her own family's intimate experiences with prisons in poignant, ironic, and unromanticized tellings. She serves us multiple "straight shot, no chaser" truths. "Prison is considered so 'natural' that it is extremely hard for most people to picture everyday life without it." And as educators, we are "*either engaged in incarceration prevention or incarceration expansion*." This essay is extremely readable, quotable, and teachable. We hope you will share it widely.

In "Beginning and Ending with Black Suffering: A Meditation on and Against Racial Justice in Education," Michael Dumas directs us to think about how the suffering of Black children and youth is the hidden referent, premise, and reproductive force behind education studies. While "blackness is not analogous to any other racially marked position," Black suffering is often treated as a zero point to calibrate projects of equity and inclusion in education that quickly move away from blackness. Such moves obscure the specificity of blackness in favor of "a universal or more generalizable understanding of racial justice." By examining antiblack incidents in schools that make the news but are actually quite normalized events that happen every day in schools everywhere, Dumas pushes us to ask how our work is informed by or ignores Black suffering, to imagine what counts as the means and ends of justice, to imagine what constitutes "a necessary racial-cultural politics of education." Centering on the question of Black suffering steps to the side of racial justice discourse, which in fact has already stepped to the side of Black suffering. "Racial justice discourse in education proceeds past/around/on the back of Black suffering, rendering Black suffering invisible or beside the point, and, most pointedly, inconsequential." This chapter is an example of that inner angle, of how justice projects are so intimate to antiblackness yet profoundly turned away from addressing it.

In "Refusing the University," Sandy Grande offers principles and principled alternatives to the academic industrial complex. Drawing from Audra Simpson's concepts of *refusing* the colonial knowledge-production processes and mandates of the university, Grande theorizes the university as a branch of the settler state—a branch that many of us are caught by and perhaps serving, reinforcing, and profiting from. Unpacking the ways that the university invests in settler colonialism, this chapter moves quickly toward ways to refuse our own complicity in the logics of colonizing institutions. Grande offers three guiding commitments: (1) To collectivity, which necessarily involves the refusal of individualistic branding and recognition for knowledge production. (2) To reciprocity, to being answerable to the communities that writers and knowledge producers claim to belong to or claim to serve. This necessarily involves refusing the pressures of accounting for publications that are valued by the neoliberal regime. (3) To mutuality, which includes relations not bound up in capital, "that refuses exploitation at the same time it radically asserts connection, particularly to land." At the heart of this ethic of refusal and of assertion is a theorizing of justice. Indeed, Grande implies that justice projects are not so far apart, not as incommensurable as we might insist, an insight that we better appreciate when we can make the "distinction between liberal theories of *justice as recognition* and critical Indigenous theories of *justice as refusal*."

In "Towards Justice as Ontology: Disability and the Question of (In)Difference," Nirmala Erevelles disrupts ableist imaginaries of justice. Disability is often uncritically adopted as a "dead metaphor" for unacceptable political difference: e.g., a hateful politician is "mentally unstable"; the politically ignorant are "deaf" or "colorblind." It is also used as a metaphor for injustice, especially for harm caused to communities: e.g., "epidemics" of violence. Justice then becomes conceptualized as the opposite of disability. Erevelles also critiques the way in which disability studies have traditionally centered the figure of a normative disabled citizen who is not Black, female, queer, ill, or otherwise intersectionally Othered. Drawing from intersectional interventions such as crippin' queer theory and DisCrit, Erevelles then guides us through a consideration of how disability connects three important contemporary events that all take place in a single year, 2014: the police murder of Michael Brown in Ferguson, Missouri; the state-based international response to the Ebola outbreak in Guinea, Liberia, and Sierra Leone; and the poisoning of the municipal water of Flint, Michigan. In each case, Erevelles reveals how the state approach is to pathologize bodies—invoking discourses of disability and illness—and thus to quarantine and destroy those bodies in order to protect normative (white) abled bodies.

Rinaldo Walcott's chapter, "Against Social Justice and the Limits of Diversity; or Black People and Freedom" grapples with the ways that frameworks like diversity and people of color obscure the exclusion of Black people from institutions, particularly universities. Writing about the everyday elisions and habitual (and well-rehearsed) erasures of Black people and Black thought in university settings, Walcott traces the institutional disregard involved in there not being "a single institution in this nation that takes as foundational that Black people are a necessary element of that which we might make a more hopeful future." Walcott observes that little has changed over the course of his career, even as the reports, the committees, the departments, the action plans, and the linguistic sophistication have pivoted toward supposedly valuing diversity. This valuing has had little impact on the experiences of Black scholars in the academy, or the ways in which Black studies is always treated as insufficient. Walcott's chapter points precisely to the ways in which making university spaces more inclusive to non-white scholars has been unsuccessful in terms of addressing the antiblack racism that is foundational to nation-states and their universities. The justice project which offers reprieve from this is heavily influenced by the work of Sylvia Wynter (2003), in that it locates culture as the site of possibility and struggle for transformation. It is a project which considers what human can more fully mean, beyond the capitalist, antiblack formulations in which humanness is currently conscribed. This project, which Walcott calls a pure decolonial project (taking its title from Derrida's "pure hospitality"), calls for a complete refashioning of the relationships and conditions which have been produced for us by the violent expansions of European colonialism. It is a call for new imaginaries as well as new languages and relations.

"When Justice is a Lackey" opens with a quotation from the comic book, *Black Panther*, as rebooted by Ta-Nehisi Coates. In this engaging essay, Leigh Patel helps us to "ascertain the ways in which injustice may be populating justice." The indictment of 35 Black teachers in Atlanta for alleged falsification of school test score data; the ironic demonstrations by many Black high school students to reinstate a white school security officer who was dismissed for physically assaulting a Black female student; the media attention to Georgetown University's histories of enslavement, sale, and torture of Black people—Patel re-reads these and other high-profile media events to show how justice is co-opted, "entangled with, servant to, injustice." In doing so, she troubles the progressive theory of change associated with such basic ideas that "it gets better," because justice does not advance without its master, injustice. Patel critiques the linearity that is presupposed within too much of social justice education. Her skillful analysis of the injustices of justice is a meaningful intervention on approaches which are incremental or piecemeal. As an antidote, Patel offers an understanding of justice that disarticulates well-being from property. We anticipate that this will become a touchstone conversation in our field.

Our next-to-final chapter is "The Revolution Has Begun," based on what is perhaps the last keynote lecture that Métis artist, author, mother and advocate Christi Belcourt will ever deliver. Belcourt almost transcendentally locates us in our historical moment, the long season, the revolution that we are in. Connecting plant and animal nations with people nations, Belcourt's writing takes us through critique of ecological (and colonial) destruction, and reminds us of the utterly miraculous forms that life has taken. She reminds us that these are our relations, that this is the side we are fighting on. This chapter is incredibly generously written, inviting all to be part of the revolution that is already happening. And Belcourt is critically generous, no dupe to the dissimilitude of inclusion that requires compromises that we cannot and should not make. Indeed, she says that "There has been much talk about reconciliation in last few years… It is astounding to me that we are even willing to sit down and talk about reconciliation. How peaceful, dignified and beautiful Indigenous people are, that we have endured all of this, and yet are still willing to share." Belcourt unties the colonial connections between ecological destruction, resource extraction, and linguicide, and restores the connections between humans and animals of different nations with the earth, water, air, and future.

Lastly, our book has a feature for educators, learners, and book study groups. "Pedagogical Applications of Toward What Justice" is a series of teaching workshops and assignments carefully composed by Deanna Del Vecchio, Sam Spady, and Nisha Toomey as a companion to the essays in the book. This final chapter offers a wealth of multimedia resources—films, television documentaries, musicals, advertisements, Instagram collections, news and magazine articles, etc.—that cover a broad scope of topics well beyond what we could do in essay form in this volume. Just as a sampling, one activity is a "Zine Project: Representation and Mournability." Another is a "Social Justice Playlist" activity where participants deconstruct popular music, and construct their own album in order to interrogate definitions of justice and underlying theories of change. Designed for organizing/community settings as well as formal classrooms, there are other helpful approaches suggested such as options to utilize themes or theories depending on the audience. Most importantly, Del Vecchio, Spady, and Toomey design these materials with the understanding that participants are not just consumers of book theory, but active co-theorists of justice.

Inconceivable Futures are Not Inconceivable

In describing the faultlines and tensions between various (compelling, exciting) social justice projects, we emphasize that this book has no pretense of being exhaustive, or representative. It is not a comprehensive reader about the different justice projects in contemporary times. It is not a catalogue, not an almanac, not a taxonomy. Included are essays which move outside of their own terms and arguments to describe the inner angle that is created within relevant justice projects; this is the method of analysis we wish to inspire in the field through this volume.

Writing about the failures of a coalitional mobilization against an anti-Muslim charter in Quebec in addressing its own antiblackness, Délice Mugabo (2016, p. 179) argues that we must refuse coalitions with "dreams and projects which cannot imagine Black life." Debates against the anti-Muslim charter were antiblack in their inattentiveness to the lived lives of Black Muslims in Quebec, but also in their use of blackness as the bottom of a social hierarchy which this charter would likewise produce, as a contrast or foil. A Black feminist activist, Mugabo powerfully insists that "I cannot work side by side with people who are not able to imagine what joy would look like for me in a new world" (p. 179). Mugabo observes that in antiblack societies, Black people have the most to lose within such coalitions because such coalitions are premised on loss—the premise of loss of status, power, wealth, access, opportunity—so that the aggrieved group would become more like Black people, except, of course, never really Black. Coalitions and social justice battle cries based on these false equivalences will always ultimately result in violence for "those whose future is inconceivable" (p. 179).

We hold these words, "those whose future is inconceivable," close, rolling them around inside with growing resolve. It is our work, the work of our field, to highlight the ways that seemingly inconceivable futures are not inconceivable, as much as it is our corollary work to demonstrate that white supremacy and fascism have no future on these lands. The arc is always bending. What futures are possible for those whose futures are inconceivable? It is this question that blazes on the horizon, and on every page of this book.

Works Referenced

Bassichis, M., Lee, A., & Spade, D. (2011). Building an abolitionist trans and queer movement with everything we've got. In E. A. Stanley & N. Smith (Eds.), *Captive genders: Trans embodiment and the prison industrial complex* (pp. 15–40). Oakland, CA: AK Press.

Berger, D, Kaba, M., & Stein, D. (2017, August 24). What abolitionists do. *Jacobin Magazine*. Retrieved from www.jacobinmag.com/2017/08/prison-abolition-reform-mass-incarceration

Brand, D. (April, 2017). *Dionne Brand: Writing against tyranny and toward liberation.* Retrieved from www.youtube.com/watch?v=ychlzoeeIm0

Carter, M. (1951). *The hill of fire glows red.* (The Miniature Poets, 4. Georgetown, GY: Master Printer).

Davis, A. Y. (2011) *Are prisons obsolete?* New York: Seven Stories Press.

Gilmore, R. W. (2007). *Golden gulag: Prisons, surplus, crisis, and opposition in globalizing California* (Vol. 21). Berkeley, CA: University of California Press.

Hall, S. (1992/1996). Cultural studies and its theoretical legacies. In D. Morley & K.-H. Chen (Eds.), *Stuart Hall: Critical dialogues in cultural studies* (pp. 262–275). Abingdon, UK: Routledge.

Harris, C. I. (1993). Whiteness as property. *Harvard Law Review, 106*, 1707–1791.

Latty, S., Scribe, M., Peters, A., & Morgan, A. (2016). Not enough human: At the scenes of indigenous and black dispossession. *Critical Ethnic Studies, 2*(2), 129–158.

Lee, F. (2017, July 10). Kin aesthetics // Excommunicate me from the Church of Social Justice. Retrieved from www.catalystwedco.com/blog/2017/7/10/kin-aesthetics-excommunicate-me-from-the-church-of-social-justice

Meiners, E. R. (2011). Ending the school-to-prison pipeline/building abolition futures. *The Urban Review, 43*(4), 547–565.

Mugabo, D. (2016). On rocks and hard places: A reflection on antiblackness in organizing against Islamophobia. *Critical Ethnic Studies, 2*(2), 159–183.

Palacios, L. C. (2016). Killing abstractions: Indigenous women and black trans girls challenging media necropower in white settler states. *Critical Ethnic Studies, 2*(2), 35–60.

Simpson, L. B. (2016). Indigenous resurgence and co-resistance. *Critical Ethnic Studies, 2*(2), 19–34.

Tuck, E. (2009). Re-visioning action: Participatory action research and Indigenous theories of change. *The Urban Review, 41*(1), 47–65.

Tuck, E., & Fine, M (2007). Inner angles: A range of ethical responses to/with Indigenous and decolonizing theories. In N. K. Denzin & M. D. Giardina (Eds.), *Ethical futures in qualitative research: Decolonizing the politics of knowledge* (pp. 145–168). New York: Routledge.

Tuck, E., & Yang, K. W. (2012). Decolonization is not a metaphor. *Decolonization: Indigeneity, Education & Society, 1*(1), 1–40.

Tuck, E., & Yang, K. W. (Eds.). (2014). *Youth resistance research and theories of change*. New York: Routledge.

Tuck, E., & Yang, K. W. (2016). What justice wants. *Critical Ethnic Studies*, *2*(2), 1–15.

Tuck, E., & Yang, K. W. (2017). Late identity. *Critical Ethnic Studies*, *3*(1), 1–19.

Wynter, S. (2003). Unsettling the coloniality of being/power/truth/freedom: Towards the human, after man, its overrepresentation—An argument. *CR: The New Centennial Review*, *3*(3), 257–337.

1

AGAINST PRISONS AND THE PIPELINE TO THEM

Crystal T. Laura

I

FRIEND: So, how do you think you've changed since high school?

ME: Well, I've become more aware of oppressive power structures—especially jails, prisons, and the whole business of corrections—and now seek to abolish them.

FRIEND: …

I cannot, for the life of me, figure out why it is sometimes easier for us to see an impending end to the world itself than it is to see a world without prisons. Here I am, with stacks of books and articles all around me that spell out the difficult past and present of prisons, and how hopeful a prisonless future would be; and I have no doubt that what I'm reading is only a taste of the knowledge that writers have dropped on us recently.

Truth: While global competitiveness is a lingering concern for many Americans, since 2002, the United States has drawn strong criticism for leading the world in the rate of incarceration.

Truth: Approximately 2.3 million adults and 69,000 kids—overwhelmingly poor people of color—are currently locked up in the nation's prisons and jails (Pew Charitable Trusts, 2010).

Truth: The sheer numbers have prompted scholars and activists to point out and explain why the incarcerated population is so predictably drawn along lines of race, class, and gender (Alexander, 2012; Gilmore, 2007; Gottschalk, 2006; Parenti, 2008); to identify viable alternatives to incarceration (Davis, 2003, 2005); to document the exorbitant financial costs of mass imprisonment (Braman, 2009; Chesney-Lind & Mauer, 2003; Western, 2006); to highlight atrocious penal conditions (Abramsky, 2007; Rhodes, 2004); to demonstrate the obstacles faced by people convicted of crimes when reentering communities and attempting to find a job paying living wages, secure housing, get healthcare, or go back to school (Manza & Uggen, 2006; Pager, 2007); and to tell us what supports can be leveraged for those who have done time or are locked up so as to reduce the chance that they will be arrested and confined again.

So, there is no shortage of well-reasoned and researched publications about anti-prison politics, which is why I am having real trouble making sense of hesitance about the concept of prison abolition.

I have already considered the possibility that many people haven't read what I've read. Fair enough. If I'm being honest, as a professor, I know full well that scholarly work often doesn't reach beyond the walls of academic settings. But I don't think access is the problem here—not in this day and age, when a number of abolitionist professors are taking to social media and circling the globe to share their views of the subject with international news outlets, religious groups, community-based organizations, schools, and anywhere else the public may be. I think something else is up. In an introduction to her classic book, *Are Prisons Obsolete?*, Angela Davis (2003) argues that the real source of the quandary is the assumed permanence of prisons as a feature in our social scenes and in our minds. According to Davis, "prison is considered so 'natural' that it is extremely hard to imagine life without it" (p. 10). In other words, we don't lack information about abolition; we lack imagination about abolition. I suppose we have to see it to believe it.

II

In the summer of 2016, organizers pitched seven small tents in a vacant lot across the street from Chicago Police Department's Homan Square facility. Considered a "Black site," where more than 7,000 people—nearly 6,000 of them Black folks—were "disappeared" by the police, Homan Square operates as an off-the-books interrogation warehouse for the city's most vulnerable. On July 20, 2016, it became a site of protest and a tool for testing the real-world practicalities of abolition.

That day, members of the racial justice-seeking #LetUsBreathe Collective led a march through the predominantly Black community of North Lawndale to Homan Square. Along the way, #LetUsBreathe drew attention to police killings of Black people in and beyond Chicago; juxtaposed the abundance of resources doled out for policing alongside the lack of commitment to support the services needed to develop Black futures; protested a proposed "Blue Lives Matter" ordinance; and called for the immediate closure of the Black site. The march commenced at Homan Square, the entrance to which another group of activists, Black Youth Project 100, had obstructed by chaining themselves together. Combining civil disobedience with block party, #LetUsBreathe took over the vacant lot opposite Homan Square, launching an encampment they called "Freedom Square" as a daylong display of what everyday life might be like outside of the current logic and institution of policing.

Freedom Square included a store—filled with free books, clothing, and toiletries—and a canvas for community art projects. Each of the seven tents represented the resource areas to which organizers believe police funding ought to be diverted: restorative justice, education, mental health, employment, housing, arts, and nutrition. In a *Truthout* op-ed published two weeks later, #LetUsBreathe Collective co-director, Kristiana Colon (2016), described how the one-day action turned into an extended commitment:

> At the end of the night, the North Lawndale youth who had come out to enjoy the event hoped the tents meant we were staying overnight and excitedly asked if they could camp with us. We weren't prepared to stay that night, but felt deeply compelled by the longing for continued engagement. The move to relaunch Freedom Square as an occupation that Friday was a spontaneous decision to deploy an extreme political tactic, largely informed by the positive feedback from the North Lawndale community, especially the children.

Word of Freedom Square as an all-volunteer run and donations-based laboratory for abolitionist politics quickly spread across activist circles and news outlets far and wide.

When I came through the tent city, I was immediately struck by the presence of Black joy—kids dancing freely, neighbors breaking bread, passersby stopping to converse and sometimes stay, talk of art and love, and the radical potential of the relationships being built. There was also the Brave Space Agreements—a code of conduct posted on a placard meant to guide how people treated the camp and each other in it, and also to help sort through conflicts. Colon wrote about one such experience of violent conflict, too:

> After a beautiful day including free bike repair workshops and craft projects, free food for the community, and ongoing political engagement, the occupation site devolved into chaos when adults intervened in a disagreement between kids about sharing bikes. Folks felt disrespected, and misunderstandings and continued transgressions raised tensions, even as Freedom Square organizers made their best efforts to de-escalate the situation. One woman emerged from the fight with a black eye, and several others nursed scrapes and bruises once the scuffle was finally calmed. Freedom Square's medic bandaged folks up in the First Aid tent as I began to gather the 30 or so people at the camp into a circle to debrief about the conflict. We shared collective space with each other, discussing the harms that had occurred within our community. We talked through accountability steps (steps that could be taken to address those harms). Nobody called the police.

There were other incidents and conflicts to which the Agreements, rather than police intervention, were applied—from stealing to bullying, and more. According to Colon, while Freedom Square was overwhelmingly beautiful in its aspiration, it certainly was not perfect. She wrote:

> It's messy, it's tiring, and in waves of oppressive heat, it takes a lot of self-awareness and patience to keep moment-to-moment frustrations in check. The ideology of imagining a world without police powerfully resounds in media clips, on protest signs, and in the air-conditioned comfort of organizing meetings; but at Freedom Square, activists and North Lawndale neighbors live, sleep, and labor side by side in 24-hour service to a community healing from decades of generational trauma, social divestment, and internalized violence. We don't have it all figured out, but with each passing day of the occupation, our hearts evolve as dramatically as our infrastructure. We come to the work with a deep will to be personally transformed and the courage to face down whatever violence, danger, or harm we encounter or create along the way.

The occupation lasted 41 days.

My brother, Chris, wasn't around to see Freedom Square. At 24, Chris has been locked up for nearly a half-decade in a rural Illinois prison, a six-hour drive from my home in the Windy City that I've taken a couple dozen times. Before that, he was held in Cook County Jail, where my most vivid memories of experiencing incarceration vicariously were made.

In the middle of 2002, I was nine months pregnant and, as is typical for a woman in that condition, I was hot and bothered, in and out of hormonal fits. I was also too wary of going into labor inside the jail to show up alone. So there we were, my husband, Jelani, and I, sitting behind a glass partition (after we'd been X-rayed, searched, and IDed by a gaggle of guards two or three times over) waiting for Chris to toddle in. Jelani checked his watch. He'd gotten in the habit of keeping tabs on the length of our visits, which were supposed to last a measly half an hour (a few minutes more, if we were lucky), but often we got much less. It was 5:00pm. By now, I thought, Chris's friends who had visited earlier should be midway home and my sister should be climbing into her car to make the schlep down here. We were spread out exactly as planned.

It was a hard lesson learning to coordinate visiting days. The year before, when Chris picked up his first case, my sister, my mother, and I went to the County to see about him. All the way up the Bishop Ford and Dan Ryan freeways, we said no more than a few words—we were all probably fantasizing about wringing his scrawny neck, as piping mad as we were. But when we arrived, taken aback by the whole situation, we agreed on the spot to stagger repeated visits in a constant rotation, to hang around the place all day long, if it meant we could keep him with us and out of his cell. I can recall Mom sharing our arrangement with the set of guards who took our registration. "It doesn't work like that," the big one chuckled. As soon as he said this, I realized that we were making a rookie mistake, proposing accommodations as if we were checking in at some highfalutin hotel. He dismissed it outright: "You came together; you'll see him together." My sister smacked her lips, my belly flopped, and my mother instantly turned red in the face. She tried explaining that we were new to the County, pleading—quietly, cautiously—for an exception. The little guard was nicer. He said, "I'm sorry, Miss, but there's nothing we can do." Annoyed, we huddled up and sketched the logistics of returning again the very next day. "Um," he butted in, "unfortunately, you can't come back for another week."

There is no dignity in jailhouse visits, and the first one is the worst. All that fear and frustration you've been harboring does not well up at the time of the arrest. No, not until you are trying to work the system—to navigate the impersonal, impenetrable gulag—does it take every fiber of you to prevent yourself from going off. But I doubt that's what I was thinking about at that moment. I was almost certainly picturing Chris, scared witless. He was 18 then—nine years younger than me. Lanky, with wide eyes like saucers. Funny, artistic, and sweet as pie. Easy pickings, for sure. When his name was called, we hurried toward the line forming outside the visiting room and filed in, cooperatively.

Somewhere between my introduction to County and the last time that I waddled into it, I discovered a couple more unstated givens: One, the term "visiting room" is a euphemism. The room—a congested hallway, really—seems to narrow with reckless determination that makes it hard to breathe. Whenever I'm inside, I instantly feel myself losing a sense of proportion, squeezed between the expanse of cement walls and stools bolted to the floor. Two, the stools tucked in the see-through cubicles on either end of the hallway are prime real estate, desirable because of their relative privacy, which, given the context, is obviously a valued comfort. Regulars know to rush for them, snag one, and stay put. That's just what Jelani and I did.

After five or six minutes, in shuffled a crush of banana yellow jumpsuits. The color is important. Had they been dressed in khaki, there would have been nothing remarkable to set them apart from the hundreds of other men under maximum security in my brother's division. But yellow is special, reserved for those in "PC" or protective custody; it screams for undue notice. For safety, Chris had asked to be separated from the general population, then changed his mind when he crossed paths with a guy in khaki who called him a snitch, and changed it again when someone on his deck was stabbed to death. PC was perhaps the lesser of two evils, but besides having a questionable reputation, the label brought with it a mixed bag. The "perk," for lack of a better word, was extra time bunkered in a cell.

This is not to be confused with "seg," or disciplinary segregation, colloquially known as "the hole". Apparently, that's a whole other situation. Chris once wrote me:

> I don't know if you came to see me but im in the hole. I can't get any phone calls, i don't know bout visits. I gotta be here for 10 days. It ain't no joke

down here crys. I can't leave the cell for showers or nothin and its drivin me crazy!!!"

And toward the end of the note, "I'm surrounded by killers and rapists… I don't fit in here."

There were eight brothers in yellow, all of them Black, and most around Chris's age. Chris, as always, took forever to appear. I bobbed from side to side—peeking over and through the crowd, waving my hands wildly—to make sure he knew he had company. Was I over the top? Sure, but as far as I am concerned, it was a necessary distraction. I have seen people—both inmates and visitors—come and go without connecting with one another. Blame those unfortunate occurrences on processing errors or maybe poor timing, but every now and then, somebody's son was left standing idly by, sick, scanning the room for his absent lifeline to the engaged world, while the rest of us chummed it up.

It was loud, understandably, with so many full-blown conversations happening all at once, and everybody trying to outdo everybody else. In the movies, there is a phone—an icky, worn-out phone, but a phone nonetheless. Here, we have a tiny, metal-grated opening in Plexiglas a good distance from a stool, which means that unless you're 6 feet tall and rail thin, like Chris (and quite unlike me), then sitting and chatting is nearly impossible. When Chris settled down, I stood and, folding over a ballooning midsection, brought my lips close enough to the speaker to kiss it. The rest was largely routine. I drew him out, asking him how he was doing, about the latest in the County, whether he had thought of a slick name for the baby, if he needed any books or money in his account. And when I ran out of steam, Jelani took the baton, keeping the exchange going.

Two things stick out in my memory from this visit: The first is that Chris had on a short-sleeved T-shirt underneath his County-issued digs with his tattoos (the ones that churned my stomach to find out he'd recently gotten) in full view. He hid them, with a long thermal top even in the warmth of a summer swelter, before only the most important people: his judge and our mother. He hid them from the judge so as not to feed any inflamed attitudes that would have colored his day in court. He hid them from Mom because he knew that being a grown man in the protective custody of the police wouldn't save him from her wrath. But it was Tuesday, and my mother's visits were consistently bright and early on Saturday mornings. Jelani and I did not have such powerful reach anyway, so Chris could skip the song and dance with us.

The other thing I remember is the goodbye, a sappy scene filled with such ritual and drama it could have been plucked right out of one of those prison documentaries. A guard called time, and everyone but Chris and me seemed to move with quickness. They scurried; we clung to the moment. Chris manipulated the cuffs to press his left hand to the glass, and I met it with my right. He looked me straight in the eyes and said, "I love you, sis. I miss y'all so much. I'll call you later. Answer the phone!" My mind wandered briefly to the bills I'd paid for these expensive phone calls. "Of course," I told him emphatically, "I'll be waiting, and I love you, too." Then came that familiar, agonizingly sad stare. I wanted to cry, but not in front of him. I swallowed hard, headed to the elevator to leave, and let it rip for the ride three floors down.

Earlier that spring, Chris had discovered in his cell a gift from a previous occupant: a tiny hole in the frosted window that overlooks a main street, a parking lot, and a visitors' walkway. As we left the building, I was so focused on finding the microscopic crack, that I crossed Jelani's path and lost my footing. He caught me, thank goodness, and held my hand as our gingerly stroll turned into a near crawl. Drumbeats resounded from all over; other invisible men were watching, communicating with us, too. And then I heard my brother, "I love you, Crys! Love you, Bro!" We smiled and yelled back, "We love you!" At the gate, a guard IDed us again, and with a bogus accent and a glint of sarcasm, said, "Okay, folks, y'all come back real soon." I ignored the jerk. Jelani looked at his watch. It was a quarter to 6:00pm. By the County's naive standards, we'd had a nice long visit.

III

I tend to write and speak to educators about the meaning and implications of abolition, my brother, and why both should matter to us in plain terms. For example, it's not unusual for me to share with colleagues my belief that we *educators are either engaged in incarceration prevention or incarceration expansion*. Period. Straight shot, no chaser. It is hard enough to visualize the human beings who are locked up in U.S. jails and prisons or the impact of incarceration on families and communities, let alone how educational labor may have contributed to the tragedy and how things can be otherwise. Yet, the cold facts are these: On every measure of academic attainment—earning a diploma, a GED, or some form of postsecondary education—those who are incarcerated lag behind us in the free world. They have lower literacy levels, fewer marketable skills, and a greater prevalence of disability. With regard to education and schooling, incarcerated people are often those who, from us, once needed the most, and somehow got the least. And when they come home to us, which the vast majority of incarcerated people eventually do, they will have access to even less, except the revolving door back to prison. So, I'm blunt here because the reality is just that sobering, and because, honestly, I find needlessly long and esoteric explanations of such an urgent matter unhelpful.

If I had a dime for every time I've heard an educator say the school-to-prison pipeline is beyond their control, I could probably write book chapters for a living. But I am not a full-time author. I'm a teacher—of teachers and administrators at a university, and before that, of formerly incarcerated folks at a community-based high school—and I call bullshit. I'm so sick and tired of young people being systematically screwed—their communities and schools divested from, destabilized, closed, and under heavy surveillance; their families criminalized, blamed, and trashed for it; their education leading to the streets, dead-end jobs, and permanent detention; and their good-intentioned adult allies feeling so overwhelmed by the enormity of the problem that we throw up our hands and hope for the best. Don't get me wrong. Hope is a viable resource, but what I gather from reading the research and observing the practice of disrupting the prison path is that hope must be combined with an essential daily habit: core strengthening.

If we are serious about ending student involvement with the criminal justice system, then we first ought to name that commitment for others and ourselves as a frame and guiding lens through which we do our jobs. Set the intention, and make it public.

For me—a mom of two beautiful Black boys who favor their uncle—the clearest description of what I do each day is "schoolwork as anti-prison work." Whether I am teaching a class, giving a lecture, facilitating a workshop, organizing a public event, participating in a protest, writing essays like this one, or nurturing collaborations with others who do the same, I filter decisions about how to spend my time in our field through that short phrase. Many colleagues in my circle use similar verbiage somewhat differently, though almost all of them put it in writing. Some plaster the vision for their educational practices on posters, bumper stickers, T shirts, and brightly colored sheets of paper. Some tape it to their classroom walls. Keep it on their desks. Jot it in their personal journals. Take it with them to parent-teacher conferences, staff development trainings, IEP meetings, and disciplinary hearings. As they go about doing the gazillion things that teachers and administrators are called to do, these mementos are visible reminders of the principles that crystallize and direct their efforts.

My pal, education scholar Dr. Valerie Kinloch, might call this act of deliberately tuning out noise and staying focused on disrupting the pipeline as "engaging your core." I once heard Valerie, a Pilates enthusiast, explain that a strong core—the layers of muscle in the torso—stabilize the whole body, providing a solid foundation for an effective and efficient workout. "Everything comes from the core," she said. Anatomically and, I'd argue, educationally, it's true.

For school-based educators who want to do something about losing students to incarceration, the clarity of that conviction is at our core. Creating personal policies and consistently making choices based on our core is how we build it up. Strengthen your core: train yourself to teach with a fundamental, non-negotiable goal of constantly (re)creating healthy and productive learning spaces that young people don't need to recover from.

No. School. Wounds. Let it sink in, because those monosyllabic sentences may at first seem unremarkable.

I'd bet the notion that schooling can hurt kids does not strike you as odd. We are all so accustomed to the structural violence inherent in the ways we organize and evaluate learning—relying on old school structures, norms, rituals, rules, and routines established more than a century ago—that they go unchecked. Fundamental questions about the social, political, and economic purposes of school in our society, about the restricted culture and outdated organization of our educational settings, about our limited definitions of intelligence and narrow contours of curricula, about the relationships teachers and students should but often do not establish and sustain through school, go unasked. In *Wounded by School*, author Kirsten Olsen (2009) takes it there, allowing us to hear people telling deeply emotional stories of their natural fire to learn being smothered before our eyes. Olsen's narrators help us name a variety of common "learning lacerations" as such and come to terms with their consequences, perhaps the most pernicious of which are lifelong.

Every day, as Olsen points out, students are taught to believe that they are not smart; that they do not have what it takes to succeed in school (and by implication, life); that their ideas lack value or validity; that their efforts, no matter how hard they try, are substandard; that they are somehow deficient, dysfunctional, and disabled; that they are bound not for college or gainful employment or full participation in our democracy, but instead for the streets, jails, and prisons. These are all unnatural disasters that we can work against—actively and in concrete ways, if only we'd so choose.

I, for one, wish you would.

Works Referenced

Abramsky, S. (2007). *American furies: Crime, punishment, and vengeance in the age of mass imprisonment*. New York: Beacon.

Alexander, M. (2012). *The new Jim Crow: Mass incarceration in the age of colorblindness*. New York: New Press.

Braman, D. (2009). *Doing time on the outside: Incarceration and family life in urban America*. Ann Arbor, MI: University of Michigan Press.

Chesney-Lind, M., & Mauer, M. (2003). *Invisible punishment: The collateral consequences of mass imprisonment*. New York: New Press.

Colon, K. R. (2016). At Freedom Square, the revolution lives in brave relationships. Retrieved from www.truth-out.org/opinion/item/37132-at-freedom-square-the-revolution-lives-in-brave-relationships

Davis, A.Y. (2003). *Are prisons obsolete?* New York: Seven Stories Press.

Davis, A.Y. (2005). *Abolition democracy: Beyond empire, prisons, and torture*. New York: Seven Stories Press.

Gilmore, R. W. (2007). *Golden gulag: Prisons, surplus, crisis, and opposition in globalizing California*. Oakland, CA: University of California Press.

Gottschalk, M. (2006). *The prison and the gallows: The politics of mass incarceration in America*. Cambridge: Cambridge University Press.

Manza, J., & Uggen, C. (2006). *Locked out: Felon disenfranchisement and American democracy*. Oxford: Oxford University Press.

Olson, K. (2009). *Wounded by school: Recapturing the joy in learning and standing up to old school culture*. New York: Teachers College, Columbia University.

Pager, D. (2007). *Marked: Race, crime, and finding work in an era of mass incarceration*. Chicago, IL: University of Chicago Press.

Parenti, C. (2008). *Lockdown America: Police and prisons in the age of crisis*. New York: Verso Press.

Pew Charitable Trusts. (2010). Collateral costs: Incarceration's effect on economic mobility. Retrieved from www.pewtrusts.org/~/media/legacy/uploadedfiles/pcs_assets/2010/collateralcosts1pdf.pdf

Rhodes, L. A. (2004). *Total confinement: Madness and reason in the maximum security prison.* Oakland, CA: University of California Press.

Western, B. (2006). *Punishment and inequality in America.* New York: Russell Sage Foundation Publications.

2

BEGINNING AND ENDING WITH BLACK SUFFERING

A Meditation on and against Racial Justice in Education

Michael J. Dumas

I can only imagine that the handcuffs chafed his wrists. As the police officer led young Ryan Turk out of the cafeteria, the 14-year-old Black boy's arms constrained behind his back, the cold metal must have pressed unyieldingly against flesh and bone. Moments before, Ryan had sat down to eat his lunch, only to remember that he had forgotten his milk, normally 65 cents but free to students like him, who are on the school's lunch program. So he rushed back to the counter, picked up a carton and began to make his way back to the table.

This is when a police officer appeared suddenly from a nearby room, grabbed his arm, and accused him of stealing the milk. Ryan strained against the cop's firm grasp, telling him, "Get off me; you're not my dad!" (Ng, 2016, May 24). I imagine that Ryan's words made the cop angry. Once in handcuffs, all it would take is a subtle, sharp jerk of Ryan's arm, enough to make the boy wince in pain. No one would call it excessive. No one would know.

Ryan was taken to the principal's office, where he was searched for drugs, and then suspended from school for theft, disrespect, and use of a cell phone. In addition, the police charged Ryan with larceny for the "theft" of the milk, and ordered him to appear in juvenile court to answer the charges.

What happened—what *is* happening—to Ryan Turk and so many other Black children in schools is the subject of a range of justice-centered scholarship on race and education. For scholars who focus on the educational experiences and academic outcomes of Black young men and boys, the aim is to address what scholars understand as the unique social, cultural, and pedagogical needs of Black males in schools in which they are often viewed as violent, perpetually in crisis, and difficult to educate (Brown, 2011; Howard, 2013). Research on racial disparities in school discipline highlights how racial bias contributes to greater surveillance of, and more severe infractions against, Black students, across gender (Skiba, Michael,

Nardo, & Peterson, 2002). Related inquiry on restorative justice practices empha-
sizes the need for interventions that invite Black boys and other students placed at
the margins to participate in the development and implementation of community
standards in ways that purportedly "restore" these students to a healthy relationship
with(in) their communities (Gonzalez, 2012). And to the extent that researchers
employ critical race theory, their analyses offer explanation of how the structures
and logics of white supremacy are implicated in the construction, implementation,
and evaluation of education policy and practice (Gillborn, 2005; Howard, 2008).
The primary aim of all of this research is to offer policy makers, education leaders,
teachers, and community advocates specific recommendations—policy propos-
als, pedagogical and relational approaches, models for professional development
of cultural competencies—intended to remedy racial inequities and improve the
educational and life chances of, in this case, Black males, often as part of a broader
project focused on creating schools committed to equity, diversity, and inclusion.

In this chapter, I want to center the question of Black suffering as a way to
engage and refuse the notion of racial justice in education. I offer an explanation
of suffering in the Black lived experience of antiblackness—not as the totality of
Black lived experience, but certainly as the ever-present condition of Black life
and sociality. Then, using recent incidents of antiblackness in and around schools,
I explain how racial justice discourse in education proceeds past/around/on the
back of Black suffering, rendering Black suffering invisible or beside the point,
and, most pointedly, inconsequential. Here, I do not mean merely that Black suffering is seen as unimportant, but that it has little to no *consequence* for how we
imagine our work, and for what counts as the means and ends of justice, or a
necessary racial-cultural politics of education. Finally, I want to wrestle with what
it might mean to begin and, in some way, end with Black suffering. I argue that
centering Black suffering as a constant meditation and inspiration for education
research and practice leads us toward clarity about what liberatory imaginations
beyond racial justice might be, must be. So here, I mean to suggest Black suffering
as a constant meditation, an ongoing remembering, an ever-present motivation for
and instigation of our interventions. In this sense, there is *no end* to our consideration of Black suffering. Actually, I go further, to insist that there is no end to Black
suffering in schools, in our current racial order, which necessitates the ongoing
suffering of Black people. Following on from this, I propose that what counts as
justice in education in no way promises an end to Black suffering. It may alleviate
or mitigate some suffering for some Black students in some educational spaces,
but the vast majority of Black children and their families will still continue to
experience suffering, even as educators and policy makers and the broader public
celebrate successes in this or that racial justice initiative.

Education is an *applied* field. This means that the expectation—both inside and
outside of the profession—is that scholarship makes a measurable difference in the
lives of children, institutions, communities, and nation-states. Although scholars
are given some space to explore the meaning of education (and even, in keeping

with the aims of this book, the meaning of justice in education), primarily we are mandated to figure out what to *do* to expand opportunities, to enrich experiences, to improve outcomes, to intervene in ways that *end* inequities. And generally, we accept that charge. We *want* to make a difference, whatever that may mean; we see ourselves as advocates, at very least, and often as activists. The applied nature of our field also means that the emphasis is on improving the systems that are already in place. In fact, I would argue that in most education scholarship, there is an implicit assumption that public education and, more specifically, public schools are generally a social good with the potential to improve society for all (Noguera, 2003). Our primary task as researchers, then, is to identify (and in many cases, quantify) those interventions that will allow the system to function as it is *already* designed to do, or at least, as many of us assume it has the possibility to do, in some ideal formation that is in our grasp if we only implement the ideal policies, appoint effective leaders, and teach the right competencies and techniques. This is the hegemonic liberal frame of education research, although it has more recently been infected with the *neo*liberal impulse to rely on market forces and logics to bring about reforms (Apple, 2011; Au & Ferrare, 2015). Even in scholarship that might be described as ideologically critical or left, there is an enduring hope that schools can be transformed into spaces of freedom, of radical possibility (Anyon, 2014). It is largely expected that our publications will end with clearly enumerated recommendations for policy and practice.

For scholars committed to racial justice in education, this has traditionally been the work: not to dismantle or destroy the system, but to seek redress, largely through contributing to deliberation within civil society, and also through interventions with/in the state itself, through partnerships with local districts and schools, and through participating in research and policy development at the state and federal levels. We call this seeking an *end* to injustice, but that is not what our work is designed to do; that is not what an antiblack society is interested in. Thus, we are rewarded for doing far, far less—something beneficial, perhaps, but not anything that ends Black suffering.

And this brings me back to Ryan Turk, sitting in the principal's office, wincing at the tug of his handcuffs, confused that he is even in this place at this moment, his stomach rumbling as his unfinished lunch sits on a table back in the cafeteria. How is our work *applied* to him? Not in the abstract sense that systemic improvements in educational conditions might benefit other young Black boys, but in the material, enfleshed sense. How do we stop Ryan's wrists from hurting? I suppose the more precise question is, *how is Ryan applied to our praxis of scholarly inquiry?* That is, how might the intentions and trajectories of our work be motivated by the materiality of Ryan's lived experiences, and an insistence on his freedom, more than—*rather than*—by the economic and social imperatives of the nation-state, the technical-managerial chase for more effective education policies, or even the pursuit of racial justice. Such pursuits are wrapped up in appealing for recognition and citizenship rights within a public sphere in which whiteness is property, and serves as the basis for legal and cultural claim to accumulation of Indigenous land and Black bodies (Grande, 2015; Harris, 1993).

Understanding Black suffering as an imperative for critical praxis may help us to avoid the tendency to "reinforce the spectacular character of Black suffering," as Saidiya Hartman (1997, p. 3) has explained it. That is, there is a danger in detailing—as I do here, to some extent—the violence wreaked against Black bodies, the beating and beating down of Black flesh and Black joy. Hartman cautions that the details of Black suffering, rather than instigating an ameliorative response to Black pleas for redress, can actually feed a desire for more details, a need for evidence of ever more egregious cruelty to somehow convince a public that Black people do indeed suffer. Even when it might be said that such evidence leads to greater self-reflection, Hartman contends, this happens at the expense of attention to Black suffering, because those who are so moved merely exchange the suffering Black body with their own. Suffering only becomes legible when they can imagine their own *non*-Black body suffering. How, Hartman asks, "does one give expression to these outrages without exacerbating the indifference to suffering that is the consequence of the benumbing spectacle or contend with the narcissistic identification that obliterates the other or the prurience that too often is the response to such displays?" (p. 4). In her work, she has chosen to meditate on the quotidian forms of Black suffering—the everyday, mundane terrors—rather than the most titillating, blood-curdling accounts. Here, I challenge us to take up Hartman's broader questions: how do we as education researchers (and practitioners) participate in these "scenes of subjection"? What are our responsibilities in and to these moments? How do we serve as witnesses to Black suffering in ways that draw our attention, not merely to flayed flesh, but to Black life lived in the face of antiblack terror in schools and other educational sites?

Although I aim to contribute to a broader discussion on the meaning of racial justice in education, I focus specifically on the Black condition and on Black suffering. I am clear that we cannot simply extrapolate from analysis of Black people to all people of color. At the same time, I believe that blackness is not analogous to any other racially marked position, and that attempts to put forth a universal or more generalizable understanding of racial justice often fall into a facile multiculturalism in which the specificity of blackness is obscured in an attempt to "move beyond" the so-called Black-white binary and foreground only those characteristics of racism that apply to all peoples of color. With Scot Nakagawa (2012), I contend that while all people of color experience racism, blackness is the fulcrum of white supremacy. That is, in the white supremacist imagination, blackness is positioned at the opposite end of whiteness, and plays the primary pivotal role in the discursive and material operationalization of race and racism. As Sylvia Wynter (1994) explains, the color line, as WEB DuBois described it, "is made fixed and invariant by the institutionally determined differential between *Whites* (as the bearers of the ostensibly highest degrees of *eugenic descent*), and *Blacks* (as the bearers of the ostensibly lowest degrees of *eugenic descent)*" (p. 51; italics in original). Precisely because of the unique and binary relationship between blackness and whiteness, and the centrality of the white-Black, Master-Slave relationship in the United States, examination of the Black condition under white supremacy—that is, the condition of Black suffering—opens up space for a more incisive critique of race, and creates a necessary foundation for the necessary work of troubling the very concept of "racial justice." In my mind, what is required for Black people to live free is not racial justice, but a commitment to Black emancipation. In fact, as I will argue here, the pursuit of racial justice in education may serve to impede the freedom of Black people, and only reproduce and reinscribe Black suffering. What we need to envision, ultimately, is an end to all of this: the destruction of the very conditions of Black suffering, which is, necessarily, the end of schooling as we understand it and, in the meantime, a perpetual troubling of what gets celebrated as racial justice in education, what is imagined as the (just) ends of our work in the field.

Imagining Antiblackness: A Theoretical Note

The position of the Black as Slave (and the white as Master) is established in the Middle Passage, through dispossessing Black people of their own bodies, and through accumulating the Black as chattel (Hartman, 1997; Sharpe, 2016; Spillers, 1987). In this sense, Black becomes synonymous with Slave, intended not only for labor, but also to satisfy every desire of whites—economic, libidinal, social, existential. What counts as the public sphere, or technologies of democracy and equality, are founded on the dispossession of Black bodies, such that the world as we know it is constructed through the position of the Black as Not Human, or Anti-Human, "against which," as Frank Wilderson (2010, p. 11) notes, "Humanity establishes, maintains, and renews its coherence." This is what is meant by Black suffering: the ontological position of the Black as having no Human place in the world. If the current social movement asserts that "Black lives matter," it is in the face of (and against) a social world in which it is impossible for Black lives to matter, because Black people are not imagined to have (their own) lives at all, let alone lives that might matter.

Saidiya Hartman (1997, p. 58) argues that the very utterance, "Black," already speaks "the sheer weight of a history of terror... inseparable from the tortured body of the enslaved."

> It acts as a reminder of the material effects of power on bodies and as an injunction to remember that the performance of blackness is inseparable from the brute force that brands, rapes, and tears open the flesh in the racial inscription of the body.
>
> *(Hartman, 1997, p. 58)*

Black, then, becomes constitutive of suffering, and the suffering of the Black is a constant testimony to the "still-unfolding narrative of the capitivity, dispossession, and domination that engenders the black subject in the Americas" (Hartman, 1997, p. 51).

In this context, the Black body is imagined as being able to withstand greater pain than non-Black bodies, and white bodies in particular. If the Black body is not fully, or really, Human, then it can be subjected to pain beyond that which is regarded as humanly possible (Hartman, 1997). Further, the Black may be seen as requiring heightened and sustained levels of pain in order to learn, as might a dog or a beast of burden. This is indicative of what Christina Sharpe (2009) has described as "monstrous intimacies," which can be understood as "master narratives of violence and forced submission that are read or reinscribed as *consent and affection*: intimacies that involve shame and trauma and their transgenerational transmission" (p. 4; emphasis added). To be clear, these most often present as "everyday mundane horrors that aren't acknowledged as horrors" (p. 3).

Too often, in education scholarship, public discourse, and even in Black cultural and political spaces, there is a tendency to dismiss attention to Black suffering as anachronistic or counterproductive, or such suffering is reduced to the conceptual frames of discrimination and disparities. In the first instance, Black suffering in schools is presumed to be something that happened "in the past"; whatever disparities or negative experiences exist in the contemporary period are imagined as "vestiges" of previous historical periods (e.g., postbellum, Jim Crow), in which racial antagonism and exclusion were more overt and sanctioned or excused by law. To the extent that analyzing Black suffering is understood as "backward-looking," it can also be seen as unhelpful in addressing the everyday needs of Black students today; in other words, even if we might acknowledge that Black students suffer in the current moment, it becomes a "waste of time" to "dwell" on it, because: 1) attention to suffering doesn't offer us actionable steps to mitigate or end the suffering; 2) it might contribute to deficit narratives, in which Black students are only described through the hardships they experience, thereby providing excuses for educators and policy makers to lower expectations for, and limit resources allocated to, Black student achievement; and 3) it might lead Black students to feel less hopeful about their own academic and life chances, due to perceptions that the racial barriers they face are ultimately insurmountable (Ogbu, 2003).

Finally, with discrimination and disparities being the most prominent frames for the study of racial injustice in education, the study of Black suffering becomes that much more marginalized. It is easier to imagine how we might act to quantifiably reduce racial discrimination and disparities than it is to effect the end of Black suffering. Moreover, I would argue that it is possible to commit to combating racial discrimination and disparities with very little interest in Black freedom, which would necessitate a reordering of a society based so heavily on the dehumanization of Black people. Put another way, we live in a society in which racial discrimination can be regarded as immoral, while Black suffering is deemed legible and even desirable. Thus, scholarly and public concern about racial discrimination or racial disparities—without situating these phenomena within the larger condition of Black suffering—obfuscates and even legitimizes the ongoing project of violence against the Black.

My interest here is not in endless theoretical abstraction, but a deeper meditation on what it is for Black people to suffer the inherent antiblackness of U.S. schooling, and then, through that meditation, to come to a deeper understanding of what Black freedom wants, what Black freedom requires of us, as we do our work in and around schools. By freedom, I mean to evoke the ideas of emancipation, of liberation, of the abolition of slavery, or at the very least, a decision to run away to somewhere, anywhere, far away from here. This cannot fit into an institutional plan, because it necessitates the dismantling of those institutions; freedom is the disordering of the Master's institutions, the reimagining of every plan the Master ever had.

Gazing Past Black Suffering in Education

Each story of a Black person who is subjected to antiblack terror is a heaviness in Black life. To read news accounts, to watch the videos, to consider how much this or that person who has been assaulted, asphyxiated, shot looks like a loved one or a friend, to say to oneself: *This could have been me.* All of this weighs on the heart, aches the body. It is then another level of psychic devastation to see how the terrorized are represented in media accounts, the choices made about what story to tell about them, and then, most dishearteningly, the quick turn to doubt the truth of what they have experienced: what were they wearing? Why did they not comply? Well, it could have been a gun.

In this section, I highlight three recent cases of Black suffering in and around schools. Although Black teachers (Pabon, 2016) and Black parents and educators (Dumas, 2014) also experience schooling as a site of Black suffering, here I focus on stories that involve Black children, not only because they are the most vulnerable to violence from adults, but also because presumably they would be the ones perceived as the most innocent and least culpable for the assaults on their own bodies. I am interested in how these incidents of suffering are represented in popular media, and the (limited) extent to which space is offered to meditate on the experiences and desires of the children themselves. It is beyond the scope of this paper to make any empirical claims about the content of the public discourse. Rather, in sharing these stories, I want to note what is most heavy, what should weigh heavily, and then reflect on what a racial justice frame too often offers as a distraction from this suffering, in ways that effectively explain away the antiblackness that is the condition of Black (children's) lives.

The Assault on Shakara at Spring Valley High

The video shows Richland County (SC) deputy Ben Fields yanking a Black girl out of her desk by her throat and slamming her against the hard classroom floor, as classmates watch in horror. The girl is known only as Shakara, and moments before, she had glanced at her phone, and then apologized to her teacher for doing so. The teacher asked her to leave the room, and when she refused, he called an administrator. She refused again, and the police officer, Fields, was called. He told Shakara she was under arrest for creating a disturbance and disobeying school rules. When she refused to get out of her seat, the 300-pound deputy immediately began his assault, which resulted in injuries to Shakara's arm, neck, and back. Deputy Fields was suspended and later fired. Shakara was charged, along with another student, who is still awaiting a court date on a charge of urging her classmates to join her in recording the assault (Jarvie, 2015; Love, 2015).

As expected, the incident led to public debate over Shakara's culpability in the police officer's attack and, more broadly, the treatment of Black people at the hands of the police. Among educators, the primary concern was racially disproportionate school discipline policies and, to a lesser extent, the role of policing in schools. The question of racial justice in this case centered largely around whether policies were administered fairly and equitably, and the possibility of restorative justice interventions that might prevent conflicts from escalating in such a violent and racially disparate way. These are all worthy conversations, but, as with Ryan Turk, I am still haunted by the physical violence, what it must have felt like for this Black girl to be put in a chokehold, and to hit the ground as the desk she was sitting in came tumbling down on top of her. And aside from that, we learn that Shakara was living in a foster home, having recently endured the death of her own mother. As Black feminist theorist and activist Barbara Smith pointed out at a recent conference at UCLA (Jacobs et al., 2017), this loss alone, and the likely lack of counseling services available to poor children in public schools, only compounds the trauma that is being wreaked upon her Black body by the white officer, in full view of her classmates. Meditate on Shakara's pain. Feel the heaviness of antiblackness as experienced in her body and spirit. And yet, here she is, wanting to stay in class. Wanting to be in school. Meditate on that as well.

"Go to the Calm-down Chair": Berating First Graders at a New York Charter School

"Count again," Charlotte Dial instructed her first-grade class, "making sure you're counting correctly." She paused and then, looking coldly at one dark-skinned girl (whose face is blurred in the video), gave a one-word order: "Count."

The child began: "1… 2—"

Dial, who is white, abruptly interrupted the child by ripping up a sheet of paper in her face. Looking down at her, she pointed to the far side of the room.

"Go to the calm-down chair and sit!" she says loudly. As the child scurried away, Dial continued, "There's nothing that infuriates me more than when you don't do what's on your paper." Turning to the other children seated on the floor beneath her, she commanded, "Somebody. Come up and show *me* how she should have counted to get her answer…"

Another student completed the problem correctly. "Thank you," Dial said sternly. She then continued to scold the little dark girl across the room: "Do *not* go back to your seat and show me one thing, and then don't do it here. You're confusing everybody! Very upset and very disappointed."

Video of this encounter at a New York City Success Academy charter school went viral after an assistant teacher gave the surreptitious recording to *The New York Times* (Taylor, 2016). She had been troubled by the consistency of the teacher's harsh treatment of the young children in her class, and hoped that others would be repulsed as well. A number of former Success Academy parents came forward to confirm that the school intentionally used such militaristic tactics intended to break the students. Current parents, organized by school CEO Eva Moskowitz to speak in favor of the school at a press conference, praised Dial and the school's efforts overall, which, in their view, curbed discipline problems and led to high standardized test scores. "I'm tired of apologizing," Moskowitz said. Dismissing Dial's behavior as "an unfortunate moment" caught on video, she explained, "Frustration is a human emotion. When you care about your students so much… and you want them to go to college and graduate, it can be frustrating" (Disare, 2016). In Moskowitz's response, and in much of the public discourse, the justification for the white teacher's behavior centers on the teacher's innate goodness, and intention to prepare children for advanced education and the world of work. We are supposed to understand that she is selflessly devoted to these dark, underprivileged children, and that their condition is so severe, so damaged, that extraordinary measures become necessary. The verbal assault on the children is described as unfortunate and as merely a "moment," as if any such moment would be regarded as tolerable if the video had featured a class full of white children. Here, the suffering of dark children disappears, as if it is not possible; to the extent that these children might be seen to suffer, it is deemed necessary, for their own good.

Antiblackness positions dark bodies as already bad; *to be Black is to be always bad*, and to be in urgent need of disciplining, punishing whiteness. What these children experience are the "everyday mundane horrors" of Sharpe's monstrous intimacies, seemingly well-meaning acts of violence that get foregrounded in an analysis of Black suffering in schools but may too easily be explained away in racial justice initiatives. By understanding this incident as an instantiation of antiblackness, rather than simply a failure of pedagogy, we create opportunities to move past consideration of pedagogical or curricular remedy to a deeper engagement with the question of Black freedom (and necessarily then, also Black bondage). What might it feel like to be trapped in this violent classroom at the age of 6 or 7, or, for that matter, at the age of 17 or 70? How do we begin to know?

The End of Dreads, Braids, and Unkempt Afros: An "Intervention" by Steve Harvey and the United States Army

This third incident began online, with a tweet from Steve Perry, a frequent media commentator, and founder of a successful charter school known for its harsh disciplinary policies. Attending a camp for Black boys sponsored by celebrity Steve Harvey, Perry witnessed a presentation by Harvey and the United States Army, a co-sponsor of the camp. Perry (2016a) tweeted: "I witnessed 200 boys VOLUNTARILY cut dreads, braids & unkept frosh bc @IAmSteveHarvey @ USArmy connected aesthetics to success. Powerful." [note: "unkept frosh" is a typographical error for "unkempt afros" and "bc" is short for "because"]. For Perry, the boys made the admirable choice to cut off Black hairstyles that might be deemed objectionable to future employers, and therefore preclude social and economic advancement. Critics of Perry's tweet countered that Black people should not be ashamed of their own hair; rather, we should be challenging dominant cultural aesthetics that deem Black hair as dirty, savage, and unprofessional. Perry responded to his critics with another tweet, "How about realizing that if hair is what makes you Black you need to learn more about Blackness" (Perry, 2016b). Of course, no one argued that specific ways of wearing kinky and curly hair *make* one Black, only that the disgust and disdain for these ways of wearing African hair are rooted firmly in antiblackness. The debate continued from there, back and forth, with Perry and his defenders arguing that they are committed to maximizing the possibilities of success for Black boys and young men, and opponents insisting that Perry is complicit in antiblack oppression, in the form of a "respectability politics" that demands Black people denounce Black aesthetics and expressions in order to placate white fears and anxieties and thereby gain social recognition. Again, this is an important exchange on what counts as racial justice, and its relationship to social mobility in the United States. That is, is Black achievement, regardless of the means or effects, an inherent indicator of racial progress? In education, is our primary aim to improve the test scores and graduation rates of Black children, or are there other aims, larger cultural-political aims of Black education that should take precedence?

Here, however, I want to meditate on Perry's assertion that these 200 boys cut off their kinks and curls and twists of African hair *voluntarily*. By their own choice. To be sure, they may have all been swayed by the argument made by Harvey and U.S. Army officials that their hair was an impediment to their futures. However, it is also true that they may have been shamed or guilted into consenting to have their hair cut. It might have been the fact that Harvey covered the cost of attending the camp, which is targeted at Black boys of single mothers, and the boys' benefactor clearly expressed the view that certain Black hairstyles were unacceptable to him. It may have been that, given the co-sponsorship of the U.S. Army, some boys may have felt pressure to impress the employer who promised them one of the few pathways to social mobility.

And, of course, Harvey, Perry, and the U.S. Army representatives are all dynamic, domineering presences, and know how to create just the right amount of fear and sadness to lead the boys to line up for what we can only imagine were a number of barbers waiting, clippers and shears in hand, for the anticipated "powerful" outcome.

This is a different form of Black suffering than in the previous two cases. It may be more difficult to see that an injustice is being done. And if we imagine that all the boys decided *en masse* to cut off their locks, braids, and afros, one might be slow to describe this as a violence committed against them. However, Black suffering also takes the form of aesthetic assault, in which the Black body is constructed as wrong, inappropriate, not enough. I want to make space for the possibility that Black children might find a decidedly Black joy in the way their hair reaches and refuses a dominant notion of order, just as there is Black joy in specific shared uses of language or movement. Thus, to the extent that Black children are forbidden access to these forms of joy, we must understand this as a form of Black suffering, as the practice of violence against the Black. The broader point of this section is to illustrate that a racial justice framing is limited in its ability to account for this more expansive understanding of Black freedom. Worse, racial justice—absent a larger imagination of and desire for Black freedom—becomes just another space within which to enact antiblackness.

Breaking: A Series of Violent Disruptions

I am writing this here because I want it to rip through this paper like so many bullets. It doesn't belong here. Perhaps in an afterword, if at all. But not here.

On the morning of June 12, 2016, I awoke early, ready to continue work on this essay. Procrastinating as I usually do, I turned on my phone and checked the news. There was only one story: multiple deaths at a gay night club in Orlando, FL. My writing forgotten, I rushed to turn on the TV to hear more, to see more. A mother was crying because she did not know if her son was alive, but he had been sitting next to his boyfriend who had been severely injured, and was currently in surgery. Her son is dead, I said to myself. And she knows it. Another mother shared a series of tweets from her son: *Mommy I love you... In club they shooting... He's coming... I'm going to die.* As profiles emerged of the 49 people killed that early morning, most of the faces were brown and Black. "Calling all our Latinos, Latinas & everyone that loves a little Latin flavor!" announced a Facebook post for that night's event. "It's time to party tonight!" (Garcia, 2016). As my friend Joseph Pierce (2016) would write the very next day:

> Latino night. When you exist as a brown body, when you love, survive, as a brown body, when your body is always subject to the various modes of violence that threaten your very existence. When you are a body that should never have existed. That was never meant to survive. To thrive. What does it

matter if you can dance? If you have that space to dance?… When that space allows you to be, to move, to breathe, to become.

(Pierce, 2016, p. 133)

The people who died looked like people I know. On any given weekend, we *have* been there. We were there that night, in blood, breathing "our [last] queer breath" (Pierce, 2016. p. 135). In pain, I did not, could not write that day, and for many days to follow.

And then, on July 5, in Baton Rouge, LA, Alton Sterling was shot and killed by police. A homeless Black man and father of five, Sterling had permission to sell CDs in front of a local convenience store. The police, who shot him in the chest at point-blank range, insisted that he was going for his gun. They also confiscated the security video and hard drive from the convenience store, and detained the owner for several hours. And their own body cameras apparently stopped working during their tussle with Sterling. However, unknown to them, a community activist had been recording the encounter; when the police did not release their own video, he decided to upload it online, where it quickly went viral. That video, and another which emerged the next day, show no evidence that Sterling reached for a gun. But it is not the details of the case that matter here; it is the cold, chilling voice of the police officer, screaming at Sterling, who is pinned down on the concrete: "Hey bro, you fuckin' move, I swear to God." Moments later, shots ring out. And then we hear a woman wailing, "Oh my God, oh my God!" as another woman in the car says, "They killed this boy!" (Kopplin & Miller, 2016). My heart heaved, and I quickly turned off my computer. No, I said, I cannot take this today. And I filed Alton Sterling away in my mind, next to Eric Garner, Walter Scott, Sandra Bland, John Crawford, Natasha McKenna, and so many other Black people killed by police. I had already seen the second video, showing Sterling on the ground, bleeding from his chest. "Fuck!" yells the cop, still holding a gun aimed at the Black man's now motionless body. I must not *feel* this, I told myself; I have writing to do.

But the very next day, Philando Castile was sitting in a suburban Minneapolis Taco Bell, fresh from getting his locs done, talking to his sister about the Alton Sterling video. "Did you watch the video on Facebook of the man getting killed?" Castile had asked his sister. "No," she replied. "I didn't watch it, bro. I refuse to watch another video" (Smith, 2016, July 12). Just hours later, Castile would appear in a video of his own, slumped over in his own car, bleeding from his chest, dying, as a police officer continues to point the murder weapon at his girlfriend, Lavish Reynolds, seated next to him. "Please, officer," Reynolds says, "don't tell me you just did this to him. You shot four bullets into him, sir." Moments later, she is handcuffed and placed in the back of the police car as several officers surround Castile, who has been placed on the ground at the side of the road. "Please don't tell me he's gone. Please, Jesus, no!" At this moment, we hear the voice of Reynold's 4-year-old daughter, who has witnessed the entire ordeal: "It's ok. I'm right here with you." We would later learn that Castile had been pulled over for an alleged broken taillight, but that was a cover; the officer had believed he fit the description of a robbery subject, because of his "wide-set nose." (Helm, 2016). The (Black) shape of his nose. I knew this would be another day, or two, or three of not writing.

To meditate on this Black suffering is to see the blood-soaked shirt, the barrel of the gun, the last twitches of an arm; it is to still hear the sound of the bullets, the desperate cries of witnesses, the police huddled together plotting their next move. It is also to remember the joy of making that CD sale that will allow you to buy a small gift for your children, the peace in knowing that your children love you regardless, the laughter with loved ones just before the red and blue lights in the rear-view mirror, the satisfying feeling from earlier in the day when you had just gotten your hair *did*. To research and write about Black suffering is to engage in a constant meditation on Black death, and the simultaneous impossibility and possibility of Black life. It is to attempt to understand the dance, and the end of dancing.

Beginning and Ending with Black Suffering

Educational research on racial justice is, almost implicitly, an appeal for redress of legal and social grievances. It is an offering toward public deliberation on schooling, opportunity, inclusion, and mobility within the antiblack social world. With regard to Black education, racial justice scholarship might be imagined as part of a negotiation with the state and civil society in an attempt to secure (the possibility of) Black freedom. Given that the social world around us is complicit in, and desirous of, perpetual antiblack violence, consideration of Black suffering becomes illegible, a threat to the antiblackness by which the world—everything which is not Black—knows itself.

Anthony Farley (2008) explains the impossibility of this negotiation for racial justice:

> *Negotiation* requires the slave to pretend that it has something in common with its master. Slaves and masters have nothing in common and there is therefore nothing to negotiate. Negotiation is always already at its beginning the almost-escaped slave's surrender to its almost-former master. There are many mansions in the master's house, each filled with the beauty of yesteryear's dreams of legal emancipation.
>
> *(Farley, 2008, p. 962)*

Within mainstream discourse on racial justice in education, the continuation of Black suffering is *non-negotiable*. Black children, families, and communities must indeed continue to suffer. Thus, what counts as rigorous research, what is funded most generously, what is most likely to be rewarded, and what is politically expedient, will always be research that leaves space for some, and arguably most, Black people to suffer. Reforms are viewed as effective if they provide incremental improvements in outcomes, or offer interventions to expand opportunities to what are most often a small number of individuals from racially marginalized populations. This is what counts as racial justice in education, or at least the pathway toward racial justice we should all follow.

What is not up for public negotiation here is the (ongoing) Master-Slave relationship. That is, racial justice research in education can never challenge the actual *conditions* of our suffering, because every court in which we make our justice appeals—whether it be the legal system, electoral politics, school-district level policy implementation, or the court of public opinion—is set against Black emancipation. "The beauty of yesteryear's dreams," as Farley puts it, includes decades of racial justice research, all ending with hopes that the knowledge we put forth might lead to some improvements for (some) Black children. But the Master knows well how to house these dreams, in so many journals and conference presentations and diversity initiatives, and yet not offer us—which is to say, the vast masses of Black people—release from the material and psychic conditions of our bondage.

Christina Sharpe (2016) suggests that what we can know about slavery and its afterlife, what our research can reveal, must exceed these institutionally sanctioned approaches to epistemology and methodology. "The methods most readily available to us," Sharpe writes, "sometimes, oftentimes, force us into positions that run counter to what we know." Our knowledge comes from academic study, to be sure, but also is gained "in excess of those studies" (p. 12). Yet, many of our ways of knowing are deemed illegible and illegitimate in the academy; in our efforts to conform, we end up "doing violence to our own capacities to read, think, and imagine otherwise" (p. 13). Or, as Farley might say, we find ourselves stuck wandering the halls of the Master's mansions. "I've been trying to articulate a method of encountering a past that's not past," Sharpe explains. "A method along the lines of a sitting with, a gathering, and a tracking of phenomena that disproportionately and devastatingly affect Black peoples any and everywhere we are" (p. 13). Sharpe goes on to propose that we might embrace what it means to be "in the wake"— that is, "to occupy and be occupied by the continuing and changing present of slavery's as yet unresolved unfolding" (pp. 13–14).

And thus it is that I suggest we begin *and* end with Black suffering. Here, I began with Ryan Turk, straining against his handcuffed wrists; continued to Shakara, bruised on the floor; and then to a little Black girl crying in the corner as her white teacher snarled her disapproval; to Black boys lining up to become "men," by cutting off their natural, *and naturally un-respectable*, Black hair. And as I ended that meditation, bullets ripped through queer Black and Brown bodies, through a Black man trying to support his children, and through another Black man as his girlfriend and her daughter witnessed in horror. This does not end. There is no social justice research or remedy to end this. It is, as Sharpe reminds us, unresolved. Unfolding.

What becomes possible when we begin and end with Black suffering? First, "sitting with" Black suffering allows us to embrace anger as a way of knowing. Everything in the academy militates against this, while everything about Black death demands it. Within anger, I mean to include mourning, that Black melancholia which Salamishah Tillet (2012) has said, is "a haunting of the past but is also a reminder of the present-day racial inequities that keep African-American citizens in an indeterminate, unassimilable state as a racialized 'Other'" (p. 9). But I am interested here in thinking about mourning as generative of anger, in part because I want to refuse calls for Black people to be peaceful, forgiving, patient. We are being brutalized and killed. That is cause for sadness. But it is also a call to rage. And we must find ways to do so in our research design, in our theorizing, in our identification of research findings and implications, and in our public presentation of our scholarship.

Second, and following from this, beginning and ending with Black suffering demands an *urgency* that refuses and exceeds what can be done, what has always been done, through education reform. Our children are despised. They are miseducated. They are killing their spirits and breaking their bones, in ways new and old, and without end. When we commit to know Black suffering—to occupy and be occupied by it, as Sharpe says—our education policy debates are not places to deliberate the implementation of various reforms, but the site of contestation between those who have come to engage in futile negotiation, and those of us who have come, must come, to upend those negotiations, to call into question the very terms which the Master offers. These terms are always premised upon the idea that we should not ask for too much, too quickly. Our urgency, expressed in our scholarship and in our teaching, disrupts this temporality of never-ending gradualist reforms, and imagines another temporality marked by a refusal to wait for another day, another conference, another publication, to get to work on an otherwise world.

Third, and finally, I believe that beginning and ending with Black suffering points us toward what kihana ross and I (Dumas & ross, 2016) have called "Black liberatory fantasy," in which we delight in the possibilities of total disorder of the system which produces so much antiblack terror. Here, we do not concern ourselves with preserving institutions, or law, or "effective" practices. Rather, we realize that the only thing that can affect Black freedom is the death of whiteness, the end of the Master. This is necessarily chaotic, unthinkable, and unproductive, particularly in the eyes of those who produce Black suffering again and again. And so we imagine how we might bring this whole thing down, and rejoice in these possibilities. In this way, Black suffering can be generative of radical action. We have witnessed the furrowed brows of Black children, their hunched shoulders, their bruised bodies, and we must intervene, to protect them and to protect ourselves and our Black futures. An ongoing meditation on Black suffering moves us to think about how our projects of inquiry and community engagement are pursued under never-ending threat of death. Waking and reawakening every day, we embrace a scholarly life with an eye past justice and toward some escape from all this.

Works Referenced

Anyon, J. (2014). *Radical possibilities.* New York: Routledge.

Apple, M. W. (2011). Democratic education in neoliberal and neoconservative times. *International Studies in Sociology of Education, 21*(1), 21–31.

Au, W., & Ferrare, J. J. (Eds.). (2015). *Mapping corporate education reform: Power and policy networks in the neoliberal state.* New York: Routledge.

Brown, A. (2011). "Same old stories": The black male in social science and educational literature, 1930s to the present. *Teachers College Record, 113*(9), 2047–2079.

Disare, M. (2016, February 12). Moskowitz defends teacher shown yelling in video, calls Times coverage biased. *Chalkbeat.* Retrieved from www.chalkbeat.org/posts/ny/2016/02/12/moskowitz-defends-teacher-shown-yelling-in-video-calls-times-coverage-biased/

Dumas, M. J. (2014). Losing an arm: Schooling as a site of Black suffering. *Race, Ethnicity and Education, 17*(1), 1–29.

Dumas, M. J., & ross, k. m. (2016). "Be real Black for me": Imagining BlackCrit in education. *Urban Education, 51*, 415–442.

Farley, A. (2008). The colorline as capital accumulation. *Buffalo Law Review, 56*, 953–963.

Garcia, F. (2016, June 15). Among the Orlando shooting victims, trans Latino advocates hope their stories are told. *Independent.* Retrieved from www.independent.co.uk/news/world/americas/orlando-nightclub-shooting-transgender-latino-latina-victim-stories-a7084391.html

Gillborn, D. (2005). Education policy as an act of white supremacy: Whiteness, critical race theory and education reform. *Journal of Education Policy, 20*(4), 485–505.

Gonzalez, T. (2012). Keeping kids in schools: Restorative justice, punitive discipline, and the school to prison pipeline. *Journal of Law & Education, 41*(2), 281–336.

Grande, S. (2015). *Red pedagogy: Native American social and political thought.* Lanham, MD: Rowman & Littlefield.

Harris, C. (1993). Whiteness as property. *Harvard Law Review, 106*(8), 1707–1791.

Hartman, S. V. (1997). *Scenes of subjection.* New York: Oxford.

Helm, A. B. (2016, July 10). Report: Philando Castile was pulled over because he matched description of suspect with 'wide-set nose.' *The Root.* Retrieved from www.theroot.com/report-philando-castile-was-pulled-over-because-he-mat-1790855964

Howard, T. C. (2008). Who really cares? The disenfranchisement of African American males in preK-12 schools: A critical race theory perspective. *Teachers College Record, 110*(5), 954–985.

Howard, T. C. (2013). How does it feel to be a problem? Black male students, schools, and learning in enhancing the knowledge base to disrupt deficit frameworks. *Review of Research in Education, 37*, 54–86.

Jacobs, L., Parker, D., Nanda, J., & Smith, B. (2017, May 7). In M. Hunter (Chair), *Thinking Beyond the Gendered Parameters of Race and School Reform.* Symposium conducted at *Is Separation The Solution? A Convening to Discuss the Theory and Practice of Gender-Based School Reforms for At-Risk Students of Color.* UCLA.

Kopplin, Z., & Miller, J. (2016, July 7). New video emerges of Alton Sterling being killed by Baton Rouge police. *The Daily Beast.* Retrieved from www.thedailybeast.com/new-video-emerges-of-alton-sterling-being-killed-by-baton-rouge-police

Love, D. (2015, October 31). Her name is Shakara: Spring Valley High victim refused to comply with unfair punishment, as 100 students stage walkout for fired deputy. *Atlanta Black Star*. Retrieved from http://atlantablackstar.com/2015/10/31/her-name-is-shakara-spring-valley-high-victim-refused-to-comply-with-unfair-punishment-as-100-students-stage-walkout-for-fired-deputy/

Nakagawa, S. (2012, May 4). Blackness is the fulcrum. Retrieved from www.racefiles.com/2012/05/04/blackness-is-the-fulcrum/

Ng, A. (2016, May 24). Virginia student arrested, suspended after being accused of stealing milk at lunch—even though it's free. *New York Daily News*. Retrieved from www.nydailynews.com/news/national/va-student-arrested-accused-stealing-free-milk-lunch-article-1.2648626

Noguera, P. (2003). *City schools and the American dream*. New York: Teachers College Press.

Ogbu, J. U. (2003). *Black American students in an affluent suburb: A study of academic disengagement*. New York: Routledge.

Pabon, A. J. M. (2016). In hindsight and now again: Black male teachers' recollections on the suffering of black male youth in US public schools. *Race Ethnicity and Education, 20*(6), 1–15.

Perry, A. (2016a, June 15). Black aesthetic, white supremacy: Steve Perry's tweet needs cutting more than Black boys' hair. *The Root*. Retrieved from www.nydailynews.com/news/national/va-student-arrested-accused-stealing-free-milk-lunch-article-1.2648626

Perry, S. (2016b, June 12). How about realizing that if hair is what makes you Black you need to learn more about Blackness. Retrieved from https://twitter.com/drsteveperry/status/742158821343268864

Pierce, J. M. (2016). Our queer breath. *QED: A Journal in GLBTQ Worldmaking, 3*(3), 133–135.

Sharpe, C. (2009). *Monstrous intimacies: Making post-slavery subjects*. Durham, NC: Duke University.

Sharpe, C. (2016). *In the wake: On blackness and being*. Durham, NC: Duke University.

Skiba, R. J., Michael, R. S., Nardo, A. C., & Peterson, R. L. (2002). The color of discipline: Sources of racial and gender disproportionality in school punishment. *The Urban Review, 34*, 317–342.

Smith, M. (2016, July 12). Philando Castile's last night: Tacos and laughs, then a drive. *The New York Times*. Retrieved from www.nytimes.com/2016/07/13/us/philando-castile-minnesota-police-shooting.html

Spillers, H. J. (1987). Mama's baby, papa's maybe: An American grammar book. *Diacritics, 17*(2), 65–81.

Taylor, K. (2016, February 12). At Success Academy School, a stumble in math and a teacher's anger on video. *The New York Times*. Retrieved from www.nytimes.com/2016/02/13/nyregion/success-academy-teacher-rips-up-student-paper.html

Tillet, S. (2012). *Sites of slavery: Citizenship and racial democracy in the post-civil rights imagination*. Durham, NC: Duke University.

Wilderson, III F. B. (2010). *Red, white & black: Cinema and the structure of US antagonisms*. Durham, NC: Duke University.

Wynter, S. (1994). No humans involved: An open letter to my colleagues. *Forum NHI, 1*(1), 42–73.

3

REFUSING THE UNIVERSITY

Sandy Grande

The fundamental problem is not that some are excluded from the hegemonic centers of the academy but that the university (as a specific institutional site) and academy (as a shifting material network) themselves cannot be disentangled from the long historical apparatuses of genocidal and protogenocidal social organization.

Dylan Rodríguez (2012, p. 812)

What happens when we refuse what all the (presumably) 'sensible' people perceive as good things? What does this refusal do to politics, to sense, to reason? When we add Indigenous peoples to this question, the assumptions and histories that structure what is perceived to be 'good' (and utilitarian goods themselves) shift… (refusal) may seem reasoned, sensible, and in fact deeply correct. Indeed, from this perspective, we see that a good is not a good for everyone.

Audra Simpson (2014, p. 1)

This analysis turns upon a theorization of the academy as *an arm of the settler state*—a site where the logics of elimination, capital accumulation, and dispossession are reconstituted—which is distinct from other frameworks that critique the academy as fundamentally neoliberal, Eurocentric, and/or patriarchal. I argue that this shift opens up more possibilities for coalition and collusion within and outside the university. I am particularly interested in examining the relationship between abolitionist and decolonial theorizations of the academy as articulated through Black radicalism and critical Indigenous studies, respectively.

Historically, the university functioned as the institutional nexus for the capitalist and religious missions of the settler state, mirroring its histories of dispossession, enslavement, exclusion, forced assimilation and integration. As noted by Craig Wilder (2014), author of *Ebony and Ivy: Race. Slavery, and the Troubled History of America's Universities*, the academy was both a "beneficiary and defender" of the same social and economic forces that "transformed the West and Central Africa through the slave trade and devastated indigenous nations in the Americas" (pp. 2–3). He writes:

> American colleges were not innocent or passive beneficiaries of conquest and colonial slavery. The European invasion of the Americas and the modern slave trade pulled peoples throughout the Atlantic world into each other's lives, and colleges were among the colonial institutions that braided their histories and rendered their fates dependent and antagonistic. The academy never stood apart from American slavery – in fact it stood beside church and state as the third pillar of a civilization built on bondage.
>
> *(Wilder, 2014, p. 11)*

Across the text, Wilder similarly registers (albeit unevenly) how the academy also never stood apart from the genocide and dispossession of Indigenous peoples. All of which illuminates the university's history as long-time accessory in the perpetuation of settler crimes against Black and Indigenous humanity.

Despite this history, student protest and charges of racism within the settler academy are often met with surprise and disbelief.[1] For example, when protests erupted in early November 2015 at the University of Missouri, they were reported as "exploding" from a series of racial "incidents" and not as a response to the relentless, decades-long, history of indiscretions of white supremacy that has characterized the campus since 1950, when the first Black student was admitted; this, despite the fact that students organized under the hashtag #ConcernedStudent1950. Months of student and faculty protests, including a hunger strike by student leader Jonathan Butler, went relatively unnoticed[2] in the national media, until the football team (players and coach) staged a boycott calling for President Tom Wolfe's resignation; the next day, Wolfe stepped down.

The students at Missouri inspired others and across the 2015–2016 academic year, students at over 80 other colleges and universities issued sets of demands, registering their shared refusal to absorb the high cost of institutional racism upon their minds and bodies.[3] Together the young people of #ConcernedStudent1950 and #BlackLivesMatter led a co-resistance movement that disabused the nation of its post-racial fantasy, exposing the apparatuses of state violence and institutional negligence predicated upon antiblack racism. As each day seems to bring a new campus disruption, it is increasingly evident that what is at stake is a fundamental condition, a structure—and not a momentary crisis or incident—an event. Which is to say, within settler societies, the university functions as an apparatus of colonization; one that refracts the "eliminative" practices, modes of governance, and forms of knowledge production that Wolfe (2006) defines as definitive of settler colonialism. All of which raises questions of whether the university-as-such is beyond reform; if it should be abolished or perhaps more mercifully "hospiced" toward a timely and apposite death (de Oliveira Andreotti, Stein, Ahenakew, & Hunt, 2015).

In his incisive essay "Black Study, Black Struggle" (2016),[4] Robin D. G. Kelley not only argues that the university is beyond reform but also that reformist strategies and politics may be complicit in the struggle against antiblack racism. He writes:

> the fully racialized social and epistemological architecture upon which the modern university is built cannot be radically transformed by 'simply' adding darker faces, safer spaces, better training, and a curriculum that acknowledges historical and contemporary oppressions. This is a bit like asking for more black police officers as a strategy to curb state violence.
>
> *(Kelley, 2016)*

As such, he is both skeptical and critical of student desires to belong—to *be of* the university—and of reform-based justice projects focused on making the university "more hospitable for Black students" (Kelley, 2016).

Kelley is clear that his intent is not to question, "the courageous students who have done more to disrupt university business-as-usual than any movement in the last century" but rather to draw attention to the "contradictory impulses within the movement," identified as "the tension between reform and revolution, between desiring to belong and rejecting the university as a cog in the neoliberal order" (Kelley, 2016). Writing from a space of both empathy and exigency, Kelley's article reads as a kind of radical-love letter to student activists, urging them to think carefully about what it means "to seek love from an institution incapable of loving them." Instead, he challenges them to (re)connect their activism to their intellectual lives and points to the long history of street-to-campus activism as well as Black scholar-activists who worked to repurpose university resources toward their own needs. He offers the Mississippi Freedom Schools, Black feminist collectives (e.g. Lessons from the Damned, 1973) and Fred Moten and Stefano Harney's (2004) theorization of the "undercommons" as examples of "fugitive spaces" where students and faculty work to cleave study and struggle, where they can be *in* but not *of* the university.

Kelley's critique of recognition-based reform projects resonates with critiques of the *politics of recognition* as articulated within critical Indigenous studies (CIS).[5] Whether through the legal apparatus of "federal recognition" or discursive petitions for acknowledgement, struggles for Indigenous sovereignty have been deeply shaped and curtailed by the politics and discourses of recognition. Rooted in liberal theories of justice, CIS scholars argue that "recognition"—as an equal right, a fiduciary obligation, a form of acknowledgement—functions as a technology of the state by which it maintains its power (as sole arbiter of recognition) and, thus, settler colonial relations (see Coulthard, 2007, 2014). In her groundbreaking book, *Mohawk Interruptus: Political Life across the Borders of Settler States*, Audra Simpson (2014) posits a *politic of refusal* as a political alternative to recognition, accounting for the multiple ways in which the Haudenosaunee generally, and Kahnawá:ke specifically, have continually refused various forms of colonial imposition from the Canadian and American governments (including citizenship), and that these refusals are constitutive of Haudenosaunee nationhood (Innes, 2015). Since the publication of this seminal text, theorizations of "refusal" have proliferated,[6] with conceptualization of the construct as a form of politics, a methodological stance, and an aesthetic.

While Kelley doesn't frame his analysis around the constructs of *recognition* and *refusal* per se, his analysis shares a common conceptual ground, particularly around the rejection of liberal theories of justice that center respect for cultural difference over critiques of power. Moreover, since Kelley wrote his essay, over 100 more Black people have been killed by police, college campuses remain a volatile terrain of struggle, and thousands of Native peoples from over 300 nations and their supporters gathered on the lands of the Oceti Sakowin in defense of water and Indigenous sovereignty. The cumulative and ongoing violences of a nation built upon Black death and Native erasure urge renewed thinking about the relationship between radical and decolonial struggles, both in and outside of the academy. I am particularly interested in examining the promissory relationship between Black radical and critical Indigenous frameworks as both help to imagine life beyond the settler state and its attendant universities. In so doing, I am aware of the tensions and antagonisms between Black and Native experience as produced through the distinct but related frameworks of white supremacy and settler colonialism. To some degree, this distinction marks the edges of the binary that marks the difference between subjectivities produced in and through relationship to land and those produced under and through significations of property.

As noted by Patrick Wolfe (2006), Black and Native peoples have been differently racialized in ways that reflect their roles in the formation of U.S. society. Since enslaved Blacks augmented settler wealth they were subject to an *expansive* racial taxonomy, codified in the "one-drop rule" whereby any amount of African ancestry made a person "Black" (i.e., more enslaved peoples = more settler wealth). At the same time, since Indigenous peoples impeded settler wealth by obstructing access to land, they were subject to a calculus of *elimination*. That is, increasing degrees of non-Indian blood or ancestry made one less "Indian" (i.e., more Indians = less settler wealth). This distinction continues to structure Black and Native experience, producing particularities that reveal the limits and aporias of both settler colonial and race theories, particularly when imposed upon each other.

Thus, while Native peoples are racialized, race is not the primary analytic of Indigenous subjectivity nor is racism the main structure of domination; that would be settler colonialism. Moreover, while questions of Native subjectivity are taken up within the fields of critical ethnic and American studies, both offer ill-fitting explanatory frameworks for Native peoples who are neither "ethnic" nor "American" but rather members of distinct tribal nations with complicated histories and relationships to both citizenship and the nation-state. At the same time, the permanence of antiblackness troubles the settler analytic, calling into question the Indigenous/settler binary and the indiscriminate folding of the experience of "racial capture and enslavement into the subject position of settler" (Day, 2015, p. 103). That said, the current manifestations of antiblackness also reveal the limits of race discourses, suggesting the need to ground analyses in the broader logics of accumulation. The above tensions and intersections demonstrate the need for greater interchange as well as raising the following questions:

- What kinds of solidarities can be developed among marginalized groups with a shared commitment to working beyond the imperatives of capital and the settler state?
- What are the critical distinctions between decolonial struggle for Indigenous sovereignty and radical justice projects for abolition, which is to say between those shaped by genocide, erasure, and dispossession and those by enslavement, exclusion, and oppression?

While the above questions guide this inquiry, I am centrally interested in how they play out on the ground, particularly in the university setting. Specifically, I aim to expand upon Kelley's analysis—his radical-love letter—by bringing it into conversation with critical Indigenous theories, offering a decolonial love letter. I draw from both theoretical frameworks as a means of thinking through how we might work "within, against, and beyond the university-as-such"—to, in effect, *refuse the university.*

Finally, given the urgencies of the moment I feel compelled to journey through Kelley's conceptual triumvirate—love, study, struggle—with even greater vigilance for places of refuge, points of co-resistance, and spaces for collective work.

Toward that end, I begin with articulating the particularities of settler colonialism and Native elimination. In the section that follows, I examine liberal theories of justice as the underlying structure operating within the politics of recognition. Next, I discuss the academy as an arm of the settler state and the ways in which it refracts settler logics and the politics of recognition. In the final section, I examine emergent scholarship on the politics of refusal as a field of possibility for building co-resistance movements between the Black radical and critical Indigenous traditions as well as others committed to refusing the settler state and its attendant institutions.

The Particularities of Settler Colonialism and Native Elimination

In contrast to other forms of colonialism, "settler colonies were not primarily established to extract surplus value from Indigenous labor" (Wolfe, 1999, p. 1) but rather were premised upon the removal of Indigenous peoples from land as a precondition of settlement. Settlers, moreover, "sought to control space, resources, and people not only by occupying land but also by establishing an exclusionary private property regime and coercive labor systems, including chattel slavery to work the land, extract resources, and build infrastructure" (Glenn, 2015, p. 54). Thus, while white supremacy, patriarchy, neoliberalism and other technologies of domination may render the contours of settler colonialism more visible (and in some ways function as co-constitutive logics), a settler colonial framework represents a particular set of relations, one that originates with the theft of Indigenous land and the "remove to replace" logics that enable that theft (Wolfe, 1999, p. 1). A logic that, in short hand, Wolfe refers to as one of elimination (Wolfe, 2006, p. 387).

As evidence of ongoing "Native elimination," consider the following: (1) that at this moment of Black Lives Matter the ongoing police violence against Indigenous peoples (killed at a higher rate than any other group)[7] has been virtually absent from public discourse; (2) that Rexdale Henry, Sarah Lee Circle Bear, Paul Castaway, Allen Locke, Joy Ann Sherman, Christina Tahhahwah, Myles Roughsurface, and Naverone Christian Landon Woods were all killed by police around the time of the street-to-campus protests but were rarely added to the running list of victims; (3) that in states with large American Indian populations, racial profiling takes the form of police targeting vehicles with reservation-issued license plates; (4) that in Canada, Indigenous peoples, particularly those who live in the more rural Western provinces, suffer higher rates of police stops, profiling, incarceration, sentencing, and killings;[8] and, (5) while the plight of missing and murdered Indigenous women in Canada has reached epidemic proportions—estimated at 4,000 over the last 30 years—it continues to receive limited attention. As a result, Native peoples across the continent have also taken to the streets with the #IdleNoMore, #AmINext, and #NoDAPL movements leading the way.

If nothing else, the Black Lives Matter and NoDAPL movements not only illustrate how, 500 years post settler invasion, Indians are still being eliminated and the "violence of slave-making" is ongoing (Wilderson, 2010, p. 54). They also substantiate the profound insight of Patrick Wolfe's (2006) apothegm that settler colonialism is a *structure* and not an *event* (p. 388). That is, beyond an event "temporally bound by the occurrence of invasion," settler colonialism is a "condition of possibility that remains formative while also changing over time," which is to say, that it is a structure (Goldstein, 2008, p. 835). This construction shifts current understanding of ongoing Black death and Native elimination from being anomalous—moments of disruption along an otherwise linear path of racial progress—to being endemic; a congenital feature of a state built upon the "entangled triad structure of settler-native-slave" (Tuck & Yang, 2012, p. 1).

For Native peoples, the structures of settler colonialism precipitate distinctive forms and modalities of Indigenous resistance. Struggle, in this context, is organized around *decolonization*—a political project that begins and ends with land and its return. As such, Tuck and Yang (2012) argue that struggles for decolonization are not simply distinct from social justice projects but rather are incommensurable. They write, "decolonization (a verb) and decolonization (a noun) cannot easily be grafted on pre-existing discourses/frameworks, even if they are critical, even if they are anti-racist, even if they are justice frameworks"[9] (p. 3). According to the authors, the difference between *decolonial* and *critical, anti-racist, justice* frameworks is that the former seeks "a change in the order of the world" while the latter desires reconciliation.[10] And, the very nature of settler colonialism precludes reconciliation.

While the authors do not parse the underlying political theory among frameworks, doing so allows for a more layered analysis of critical and/or anti-racist frameworks. If the aim is to create greater possibilities for co-resistance, it is important to consider how political theory reconfigures the broader construct of justice. It is worth questioning, for example, whether the supposed incommensurability between decolonization and other frameworks is, in part, more fundamentally underwritten by the distinction between liberal theories of *justice as recognition* and critical Indigenous theories of *justice as refusal*. While "justice" is not an Indigenous construct, the work of CIS scholars carefully parses "the network of presuppositions" that underpin *liberal* forms of "political theory, social theory and humanist ethics" from Indigenous forms and discourses (Povinelli, 2001, p. 13). Similarly, while Kelley's framework is decidedly "anti-racist," he critiques the limits of liberal race discourses and the politics of recognition, embracing instead the elements of refusal within the Black radical tradition. All of which suggests the need for closer examination of liberal political theory, state formation, and the genealogy of recognition.

Liberal Theories of Justice and the Politics of Recognition

Theories of recognition emerged in response to political processes undertaken in "transitional nation-states" (i.e. those moving from a state of war toward democracy) where demands for recognition were levied as a means of ushering in that transition (Kymlicka & Bashir, 2008, p. 3). Within this context, (state) recognition assumed many forms (e.g., truth and reconciliation commissions, reparations, formal state apologies) that are elucidated through various liberal discourses such as healing, trauma, and memory (p. 6).[11] The prevailing idea is that the recognition and affirmation of cultural difference must precede and/or serve as a precondition of relations of equality, freedom, and justice.

More recently, recognition-based politics have migrated to established Western democracies such as Australia, Canada, and the United States as increasing demands to reconcile Indigenous claims to nationhood with state sovereignty have emerged (Coulthard, 2007, p. 438). This development in Indigenous politics has drawn renewed attention to some of the classic literature on recognition (e.g., Butler, 1990; Fraser, 1997; Honneth, 1992, 1996; Kymlicka, 1995; Taylor, Gutmann, & Taylor, 1994). Though varied, these works made an important intervention in established theories of identity development, initiating a shift away from atomistic to dialogical models, which underscore the ways in which identity formation does not occur in isolation but rather through complex relations of recognition (Taylor et al., 1994). In so doing, acts of recognition—of acknowledging and respecting the status, being, and rights of another—became integral to theories of justice. Stated differently, political theories of recognition help to expose the conditions of oppression that arise when individuals are denied the equitable grounds upon which to formulate healthy notions of self as a result of a given society's dominant and exclusionary patterns of interpretation and valuation (Baum, 2004, p. 1073). Taylor et al. (1994), in particular, consider the significant impact of non-recognition and misrecognition on marginalized peoples and their potential to produce crippling forms of self-hatred. As such, he argues that "due recognition is not just a courtesy we owe people. It is a vital human need" (p. 26).

As policies and politics of recognition have come to increasingly condition Indigenous-state relations, there has been a corollary increase in scholarship examining their impact. Indigenous scholars, in particular, have developed trenchant critiques of recognition, accounting for the failure of liberal theories of justice to address asymmetries of power. In his groundbreaking text, *Red Skins, White Masks: Rejecting the Colonial Politics of Recognition*, Dene scholar Glen Coulthard (2014) builds upon the work of Fanon, arguing that while recognition draws attention to the role of misrecognition in reinforcing colonial domination, the breadth of power at play in colonial systems cannot be transcended through the mere institutionalizing of a liberal regime of mutual recognition. In short, he exposes the limits of recognition-based politics for restructuring Indigenous-state relations, as it leaves intact the state's role as arbiter and therefore ultimately reproduces the very configurations of colonial power that Native peoples seek to transcend. Indeed, given that the state emerged through the criminal acts of genocide, land dispossession, and enslavement and the legal fictions of "discovery" and "terra nullius," its own legitimacy is what should be at stake, not the sovereignty of Indigenous nations.[12]

That said, Coulthard (2014) does not dismiss the significance of the "psycho-affective attachment" to colonialist forms of recognition and the ways in which such desire is cultivated and internalized. Specifically, he points to Fanon's "painstaking" articulation of the multiple ways in which such feelings of "attachment" are cultivated among the colonized, particularly through the unequal exchange of institutionalized and interpersonal patterns of recognition between the colonial society and the marginalized. Sara Ahmed (2004) similarly theorizes the production of psychic forms of attachment or desire through what she terms the "affective economy,"[13] examining its function in the reconsolidation of the (neoliberal) nation-state. To clarify, the affective economy is one of the central mechanisms through which subjects become "invested emotionally, libidinally, and erotically" in the collective (Agathangelou et al., 2008, p. 122). In the context of Indigenous-state relations, Wolfe (2013) writes about "inducements" as a tool of the affective economy through which the desire for recognition has been cultivated. He writes, "from the treaty era onwards Indigenous peoples have been subjected to a recurrent cycle of inducements" extended in the form of allotments, citizenship, and tribal enrollment that have continuously served to entice Native peoples to "consent to their own dispossession" (p. 259). When recognition comes in the form of economic gain for individuals, Coulthard (2007) argues that it carries the potential for creating a new (Aboriginal) elite whose "thirst for profit" comes to "outweigh their ancestral obligations" (p. 452).[14] In other words, he suggests that people who are held hostage do not make "choices"—adaptation while under threat of annihilation is nothing more than a ransom demand. Agathangelou (et al.) similarly theorizes the affective economy as transpiring through what she defines as an "imperial project of promise and non-promise" (p. 128)—a process through which a series of (false) promises are granted to certain subjects that is reliant on another series of (non)promises made to (non)subjects upon whom the entire production is staged (p. 123). Her work helps us understand the ways in which revolutionary and redistributive yearnings that would challenge the foundations of the U.S. state, capital, and racial relations have been systematically replaced with strategies for individualized incorporation in the settler order.

In the following section, I graft these critiques of recognition onto Kelley's analyses of students' desire for institutional recognition. I am particularly interested in the ways in which such demands are also conditioned by and through liberal theories of justice that ultimately sustain relations of institutional oppression. I start the section with a brief history of how the academy refracts settler logics and then move on to a discussion of how such logics and history continue to be played out, particularly through the affective economy of desire.

The Settler Academy and the Politics of Recognition

It was not until the dawn of the African-American Civil Rights Movement (1954) that the underlying justification for institutional exclusion and segregation of Black students was broadly questioned as incompatible with the norms of liberal democracy. During this time, the university became one of the primary sites of struggle and social transformation. In "Black Study, Black Struggle," Kelley recounts the rich tradition of Black studies as it emerged through the "mass revolt" of "insurgent intellectuals" committed to the development of "fugitive spaces" not just outside, but also in opposition to, the Eurocentric university. He cites the works of James Baldwin, Ella Baker, Walter Rodney, Frantz Fanon, Angela Davis, Barbara Smith, C. L. R. James, and Cedric Robinson, among others, as the "sources of social critique" that helped to inspire alternative spaces like the Mississippi Freedom Schools. The aim was not simply to offer a broader, more inclusive curriculum, but rather to design one that examined power along the axes of race and class, developing "trenchant critiques of materialism" that helped to challenge "the myth that the civil rights movement was just about claiming a place in mainstream society" (Kelley, 2016). The desire, as articulated by Kelley, was not for "equal opportunity in a burning house;" rather, "they wanted to build a new house."

But since the settler university can only "remove to replace," it was not long before the revolutionary and redistributive aims of Black radicalism were supplanted by and absorbed within the political project of liberal pluralism, transposing the anti-capitalist critique with a politics of recognition. In other words, through the structures of settler logics, the demands of #ConcernedStudent1950 are only legible as the desire for recognition and more "intense inclusion" (Kelley, 2016). While demands for safe spaces, greater diversity, mental health counseling, curricular representation, and renamed campus buildings are hardly inconsequential, they also have the potential to function as inducements. Thus, just as recognition-based politics impede Indigenous struggles for decolonization, they also constrain efforts for more a radical vision for Black study and struggle within and against the university In other words, the settler state has an array of strategies—recognition being one of them—to placate dispossessed people while evading any effort to change the underlying power structure.

Despite all the handwringing by university officials, within the context of the liberal academy, discourses of recognition garner wide appeal as they provide a means for neatly bracketing what are fundamentally complex and ongoing sets of power relations. Such demands mark a definitive endpoint to a history of wrongdoing as well as a means for moving beyond that history (Corntassel & Holder, 2008). Consider, for example, the growing wave of colleges and universities seeking to reconcile their involvement in the slave trade. The University of Alabama (2004), the University of Virginia (2007), and Emory University (2011) have all issued formal apologies. The University of North Carolina at Chapel Hill erected a memorial, Washington and Lee removed all its confederate flags, and the College of William and Mary launched an investigation into its history of complicity. Brown University launched one of the most comprehensive projects that included a commissioned three-year study, an acknowledgement, a memorial, and an endowment for Providence public schools. While the symbolic importance of such projects should not be underestimated, they should also be understood as a first step toward restructuring material conditions. For example, consider that though it has been 15 years since the Brown study was launched, only 7.3% of their student body and 4% of its faculty are currently African-American. And, no institution to date has offered reparations.[15]

Nevertheless, recognition not only continues to serve as the dominant institutional framework for addressing structural racism but also, as noted by Kelley (2016, para. 7), student activists now parrot the discourses of recognition and thereby unwittingly participate in their own continued marginalization. A thematic analysis of the current compilation of student demands from across 70 institutions shows that 88% demanded either changes to curricula or diversity training (especially for faculty); 87% demanded more support for students of color (i.e., multicultural centers, residence halls, financial aid, mental health services); 79% demanded greater faculty diversity; and 24% desire apologies and acknowledgments. This breakdown suggests that the central organizing principal for demands is indeed the desire for a more "hospitable" institution. Yet, it isn't so much the nature of the demands that Kelley takes issue with but rather their persistent framing through the discourses of *personal* trauma (emphasis in original) and the potential to "slip into" thinking about "ourselves as victims and objects rather than agents" (Kelley, 2016). In some instances, faculty have joined students, sometimes issuing their own demands for recognition. Most often, faculty demands are organized around issues of tenure, the exploitation of contingent faculty, and increasing violations of academic freedom, which disproportionately impact women and faculty of color.

One of the most recent and widely celebrated texts to narrate both the struggle and political project of women of color in the academy is entitled *Presumed Incompetent: The Intersections of Race and Class for Women in Academia* (Gutiérrez y Muhs et al., 2012). According to the authors, the central aim of the text is to provide a space for women to "name their wounds in order to heal them" and their collective demand is for future generations of women of color to enjoy "more fulfilling, respectful and dignified experiences" (p. xx). The 30 personal narratives of the contributors each capture the visceral nature of racism and sexism as played out upon their bodies. The importance of putting a face to what often goes unnamed and dismissed cannot be underestimated. This underscores the effect of non- and misrecognition as not only dehumanizing but also cumulative; as Kelley notes, the "Trauma is real" (2016, para. 23). While these aims are indisputable—everyone deserves respect and dignified experiences at work—the political project seems to end there.

Among the 100-plus recommendations made in the final chapter, "Lessons from the Experience of Women of Color Working in Academia," none of them calls for collective action against the neoliberal capitalist or settler logics that situate women in asymmetric relations of power in the first place. Their main contention is not with the structures and systems of domination that gave rise to the university, but rather with women's inability to fully participate in them (and thus have access to the inducements associated with its recognition). This aim is most evident in the following passage:

> The essays in *Presumed Incompetent* point… toward the Third World Feminist recognition that the business of knowledge production, like the production of tea, spices, and bananas, has an imperialist history that it has never shaken. Inventing the postcolonial university is the task of the twenty-first century. We can only hope that this task of decolonizing American academia

is completed before the tenure track itself disappears. Otherwise scholars in the next century may confront another ironic example of women finally rising in a profession just as it loses its prestige and social value.

(Niemann, 2012, p. 499)

Ultimately, the demand for belonging and inclusion—for presumed competence—is mobilized through a politics of recognition that not only legitimates the institutions' power over women of color but also mistakes the formation of an intellectual elite (even if it is elite of color) for radical social change.

Academic Refusal and the Possibilities of Co-Resistance

In the broader field of critical theory, the work of Marcuse (1964) is central to theorizations of refusal. His central argument is that in modern capitalist societies—where worth is equated with the "reproduction of value" and "extraction of profit"—human beings only exist as "an instrumental means" of capital and, within this context, "simply to exist, *to be*, is an act of refusal" (Garland, 2013, p. 376). As such, refusal should not be confused with "passive withdrawal or retreat" but rather understood as an active instantiation of "a radically different mode-of-being and mode-of-doing" (p. 375). Frank Wilderson (2003) troubles the capitalist foundation of refusal from the standpoint of Black subjectivity. Specifically, in distinction to what he refers to as the "coherent" subjects of anti-capitalist struggle (e.g., the worker, the immigrant, the woman), Wilderson posits the "incoherence" of Black subjects (i.e., the unwaged slave, the prison slave) as destabilizing, as "the unthought" of historical materialism (pp. 21–22). He writes:

> Black liberation, as a prospect, makes radicalism more dangerous...not because it raises the specter of an alternative polity (such as socialism or community control of existing resources), but because its condition of possibility and gesture of resistance function as a negative dialectic: a politics of refusal and a refusal to affirm a "program of complete disorder."
>
> *(Wilderson, 2003, p. 26)*

Within this context, Black refusal is theorized as "an endless antagonism that cannot be satisfied (via reform or reparation)" (Wilderson, 2003, p. 26).

Taking into account the power relations of both capitalism and white supremacy, Indigenous scholars posit refusal as a positive stance that is:

> less oriented around attaining an affirmative form of recognition... and more about critically revaluating, reconstructing and redeploying culture and tradition in ways that seek to prefigure... a radical alternative to the structural and psycho-affective facets of colonial domination.
>
> *(Coulthard, 2007, p. 456)*

In this way, Indigenous refusal both negatively rejects the (false) promise of inclusion and other inducements of the settler state and positively asserts Indigenous sovereignty and peoplehood. In *Mohawk Interruptus* (2014), Audra Simpson theorizes *refusal* as distinct from resistance in that it does not take authority as a given. More specifically, at the heart of the text, she theorizes refusal at the "level of method and representation," exposing the colonialist underpinnings of the "demand to know" as a settler logic. In response, she develops the notion of *ethnographic refusal* as a stance or space for Indigenous subjects to limit access to what is knowable and to being known, articulating how refusal works "in everyday encounters to enunciate repeatedly to ourselves and to outsiders that 'this is who we are, this is who you are, these are my rights'" (Simpson, 2007, p. 73).

Mignolo (2011) and Quijano (1991) similarly take up *refusal* in relation to knowledge formation, asserting Indigenous knowledge itself as a form of refusal; a space of *epistemic disobedience* that is "delinked" from Western, liberal, capitalist understandings of knowledge as production. Gómez-Barris (2012) theorizes the Mapuche hunger strikes as "an extreme bodily performance and political instantiation" of refusal, an act wherein their starving bodies upon the land literally enact what it means to live in a state of permanent war (p. 120). Understood as expressions of sovereignty, such acts of refusal threaten the settler state, carrying dire if not deadly consequences for Indigenous subjects. As noted by Ferguson (2015), "capitalist settler states prefer resistance" because it can be "negotiated or recognized," but refusal "throws into doubt" the entire system and is therefore more dangerous.

While within the university the consequences of academic refusal are much less dire, they still carry a risk. To refuse inclusion offends institutional authorities offering "the gift" of belonging, creating conditions of precarity for the refuser. For example, refusal to participate in the politics of respectability that characterizes institutional governance can result in social isolation, administrative retribution, and struggles with self-worth. Similarly, the refusal to comply with the normative structures of tenure and promotion (e.g., emphasizing quantity over quality; publishing in "mainstream" journals) can and does lead to increased marginalization, exploitation, and job loss.[16] And, in a system where Indigenous scholars comprise less than 1% of the professorate, such consequences not only bear hardships for individuals but also whole communities. That said, academic "rewards" and inducements accessed through recognition-based politics can have even deeper consequences. As Jodi Byrd (2011) reminds us, the colonization of Indigenous lands, bodies, and minds will not be ended by "further inclusion or more participation" (Byrd, 2011, p. xxvi).

The inspirational work of Black radical and Indigenous scholars compels thinking beyond the limits of academic recognition and about the generative spaces of refusal that not only reject settler logics but also foster possibilities of co-resistance. The prospect of coalition re-raises one of the initial animating questions of this chapter: What kinds of solidarities can be developed among peoples with a shared commitment to working beyond the imperatives of capital and the settler state? Clearly, despite the ubiquitous and often overly facile calls for solidarity, building effective coalitions is deeply challenging, even among insurgent scholars. Within this particular context, tensions between Indigenous sovereignty and decolonial projects and anti-racist, social justice projects, raise a series of suspicions: whether calls for Indigenous sovereignty somehow elide the *a priori* condition of blackness (the "unsovereign" subject),[17] whether anti-racist struggles sufficiently account for Indigenous sovereignty as a land-based struggle elucidated outside regimes of property, and whether theorizations of settler colonialism sufficiently account for the forces and structures of white supremacy, racial slavery, and antiblackness.

Rather than posit such tensions as terminally incommensurable, however, I want to suggest a parallel politics of dialectical co-resistance. When Black peoples can *still* be killed but not murdered; when Indians are *still* made to disappear; when (Indigenous) land and Black bodies are still destroyed and accumulated for settler profit; it is incumbent upon all those who claim a commitment to refusing the white supremacist, capitalist, settler state, to do the hard work of building "interconnected movements for decolonization" (Coulthard, 2014). The struggle is real. It is both material and psychological, both method and politics, and thus must necessarily straddle the both/and (as opposed to either/or) coordinates of revolutionary change. In terms of process, this means working simultaneously beyond *resistance* and through the enactment of *refusal*—as fugitive, abolitionist, and Indigenous, sovereign subjects.

Within the context of the university, this means replacing calls for more inclusive and diverse, *safe spaces* within the university with the development of a network of sovereign, *safe houses* outside the university. Kelley reminds us of the long history of this struggle, recalling the Institute of the Black World at Atlanta University (1969), the Mississippi Freedom Schools, and the work of Black feminists Patricia Robinson, Donna Middleton, and Patricia Haden as inspirational models. As a contemporary model, he references Harney and Moten's vision of the undercommons as a space of possibility: a fugitive space wherein the pursuit of knowledge is not perceived as a path toward upward mobility and material wealth but rather as a means toward eradicating oppression in all of its forms (Undercommoning Collective). The ultimate goal, according to Kelley (2016), is to create in the present a future that overthrows the logic of neoliberalism. Scholars within Native studies similarly build upon a long tradition of refusing the university, theorizing from and about sovereignty through land-based models of education. Whereas a fugitive flees and seeks to escape, the Indigenous stands ground or, as Deborah Bird points out, "to get in the way of settler colonization, all the native has to do is stay at home" (as cited in Wolfe, 2006, p. 388). The ultimate goal of Indigenous refusal is Indigenous resurgence; a struggle that includes but is not limited to the return of Indigenous land.

Again, while the aims may be different (and in some sense competing), efforts toward the development of parallel projects of co-resistance are possible through vigilant and sustained engagement. The "common ground" here is not necessarily literal but rather conceptual, a corpus of shared ethics and analytics: anti-capitalist, feminist, anti-colonial. Rather than allies, we are accomplices—plotting the death but not murder of the settler university. Toward this end, I offer some additional strategies for refusing the university:

First and foremost, we need to *commit to collectivity*—to staging a refusal of the individualist promise project of the settler state and its attendant institutions. This requires that we engage in a radical and ongoing reflexivity about who we are and how we situate ourselves in the world. This includes but is not limited to a *refusal* of the cycle of individualized inducements—particularly, the awards, appointments, and grants that require complicity or allegiance to institutions that continue to oppress and dispossess. It is also a call to refuse the perceived imperative to self-promote, to brand one's work and body. This includes all the personal webpages, incessant Facebook updates, and Twitter feeds featuring our latest accomplishments, publications, grants, rewards, etc. etc. Just. Make. It. Stop. The journey is not about self—which means it is not about promotion and tenure—it is about the disruption and dismantling of those structures and processes that create hierarchies of individual worth and labor.

Second, we must *commit to reciprocity*—the kind that is primarily about being answerable to those communities we claim as our own and those we claim to serve. It is about being answerable to each other and our work. One of the many things lost to the pressures of the publish-or-perish, quantity-over-quality neoliberal regime is the loss of good critique. We have come to confuse support with sycophantic praise and critical evaluation with personal injury. Through the ethic of reciprocity, we need to remind ourselves that accountability to the collective requires a commitment to engage, extend, trouble, speak back to, and intensify our words and deeds.

Third, we need to *commit to mutuality*, which implies reciprocity but is ultimately more encompassing. It is about the development of social relations not contingent upon the imperatives of capital—that refuses exploitation at the same time as it radically asserts connection, particularly to land. Inherent to a land-based ethic is a commitment to slowness and to the arc of inter-generational resurgence and transformation. One of the many ways that the academy recapitulates colonial logics is through the overvaluing of fast, new, young, and individualist voices and the undervaluing of slow, elder, and collective ones. And in such a system, relations and paradigms of connection, mutuality, and collectivity are inevitably undermined. For Indigenous peoples, such begin and end with land, centering questions of what it means to be a good relative.

Toward this end, I have been thinking a lot lately about the formation of a new scholarly collective, one that writes and researches under a *nom de guerre*—like the Black feminist scholars and activists who wrote under and through the Combahee River Collective or the more recent collective of scholars and activists publishing as "the uncertain commons."[18] If furthering the aims of insurgence and resurgence (and not individual recognition) is what we hold paramount, then perhaps one of the most radical refusals we can authorize is to work together as one; to enact a kind of Zapatismo scholarship and a *balaclava politics* where the work of the collectivity is intentionally structured to obscure and transcend the single voice, body, and life. Together we could write in refusal of liberal, essentialist forms of identity politics, of individualist inducements, of capitalist imperatives, and other productivist logics of accumulation. This is what love as refusal looks like. It is the un-demand, the un-desire to be either *of* or *in* the university. It is the radical assertion to be *on*: land. Decolonial love is land.

Notes

1 Consider, for example, the discourse of "surprise" evident in this reporting of the protests: www.pbs.org/newshour/updates/college-newspaper-editors-on-race-and-racism-on-their-campuses/

2 The *Washington Post* reports that on the Friday prior to the announcement of the boycott, there were "a few hundred tweets about the University of Missouri" and by Sunday, there were "nearly 16,000." www.bustle.com/articles/122644-a-timeline-of-the-university-of-missouri-events-shows-the-discussion-about-campus-racism-isnt-over

3 The subsequent murders of Eric Garner, Sandra Bland, Tamir Rice, Tanisha Anderson, Walter Scott, and Rekia Boyd among others* only further kindled what became an unremitting cycle of protest moving between street and campus. *Note: I feel the necessity to mark the effort to try to keep up with the growing body count of Black men and women killed by police as I wrote and revised this chapter. As the effort proved increasingly and depressingly futile, I decided to insert the term, "among others."

4 This article appears in the *Boston Review*, an online publication that does not include page numbers. It will be referenced throughout the chapter as Kelley (2016).

5 The primary concern of CIS is Indigenous resurgence and decolonization. Toward that end, it undertakes (Western) critical theory as a means of "unmapping" the structures, processes, and discourses of settler colonialism; at the same time, it works to disrupt and redirect the matrix of presuppositions that underlie it (Byrd, 2011).

6 See, for example, a special issue of *Cultural Anthropology* dedicated to the topic: McGranahan, C. (2016). Theorizing refusal: An introduction. *Cultural Anthropology*, *31*(3), 319–325. Retrieved from https://culanth.org/articles/817-theorizing-refusal-an-introduction

7 According to a Center on Juvenile and Criminal Justice analysis of Centers of Disease Control and Prevention data, Native Americans account for 1.9% of all police killings while they make up only 0.8% of the population. In comparison, African-Americans make up 13% of the population and 26% of police killings.

8 In Saskatoon, Canada, there is also a legacy of "starlight tours" spanning roughly 1990–2010, whereby Saskatoon police officers arrested Aboriginal men, drove them out of the city, and abandoned them. The number of victims dying of hypothermia as a result of these "tours" is unknown.

9 It should be noted that the authors do not distinguish between liberal and radical justice projects in their analysis, other than to name both as incommensurable with decolonial projects.

10 Tuck and Yang (2012) clarify that reconciliation, "is about rescuing settler normalcy, about rescuing a settler future" (p. 35).

11 Consider, for example, the Truth and Reconciliation Commissions in South Africa following apartheid and in Chile after the Pinochet regime.

12 Scholar-activists of the "Undercommoning project" similarly claim that "the university has always been a thief, stealing people's labor, time and energy" and thus "charge that the university-as-such is a criminal institution." http://undercommoning.org/undercommoning-within-against-and-beyond/

13 Ahmed (2004) argues in *Affective Economies* that "emotions do things" (p. 119). Specifically, the circulation and mobilization of emotions (e.g., desire, pleasure, fear, hate) work to bind subjects with communities. In so doing, they function as a form of capital "produced only as an effect of their circulation" (p. 120).

14 For example, with regard to the promise project of gay marriage, Agathangelou, Bassichis, & Spira (2008) describe how liberal theories of justice manifest through the individual inducement of marriage (that functions as a false promise) and how this affective economy not only sustains material relations of oppression but also serves to domesticate the "gay agenda." They write: "We... locate the mobilization of highly individualized narratives of bourgeois belonging and ascension within a larger promise project that offers to some the tenuous promise of mobility, freedom, and equality. This strategy is picked up in a privatized, corporatized, and sanitized 'gay agenda' that places, for example, gay marriage and penalty-enhancing hate crime laws at the top of its priorities. It has been this promise project that has been crucial in rerouting so much of queer politics and longing from 'Stonewall to the suburbs'" (pp. 123–124).

15 After it came to public light that Georgetown University sold 272 enslaved men, women, and children (the youngest was 2 months old) back in 1838 in order to avoid bankruptcy (sale proceeds are estimated at $3.3 million in today's dollars), University alumni helped launch the "Memory Project," an initiative dedicated to tracing and locating living descendants of those sold. There has been some discussion of reparations in this particular case, but so far nothing has come to fruition.

16 According to the *Journal of Blacks in Higher Education*, Blacks make up approximately 5.2% of faculty nationwide.

17 As discussed by Jared Sexton in: Sexton, J. (2016). The *vel* of slavery: Tracking the figure of the unsovereign. *Critical Sociology, 42*(4–5), 583–597. Retrieved from http://journals.sagepub.com/doi/10.1177/0896920514552535

18 Authors writing under this *nom de guerre* recently published *Speculate This!* (Duke University Press, 2013).

Works Referenced

Agathangelou, A. M., Bassichis, D., & Spira, T. L. (2008). Intimate investments: Homonormativity, global lockdown, and seductions of empire. *Radical History Review, 100*, 120–143.

Ahmed, S. (2004). Affective economies. *Social Text, 22*(2), 117–139.

Baum, B. (2004). Feminist politics of recognition. *Signs, 29*(4), 1073–1102.

Butler, J. (1990). *Gender trouble: Feminism and the subversion of identity*. New York: Routledge.

Byrd, J. A. (2011). *The transit of empire: Indigenous critiques of colonialism*. Minneapolis, MN: University of Minnesota Press.

Corntassel, J., & Holder, C. (2008). Who's sorry now? Government apologies, truth commissions, and indigenous self-determination in Australia, Canada, Guatemala, and Peru. *Human Rights Review, 9*(4), 465–489.

Coulthard, G. S. (2007). Subjects of empire: Indigenous peoples and the 'politics of recognition' in Canada. *Contemporary Political Theory, 6*(4), 437–460.

Coulthard, G. S. (2014). *Red skin, White masks: Rejecting the colonial politics of recognition.* Minneapolis, MI: University of Minnesota Press.

Day, I. (2015). Being or nothingness: Indigeneity, antiblackness, and settler colonial critique. *Critical Ethnic Studies, 1*(2), 102–121.

de Oliveira Andreotti, V., Stein, S., Ahenakew, C., & Hunt, D. (2015). Mapping interpretations of decolonization in the context of higher education. *Decolonization: Indigeneity, Education & Society, 4*(1), 21–40.

Ferguson, K. (2015). Refusing settler colonialism: Simpson's mohawk interruptus. *Theory & Event, 18*(4), 6.

Fraser, N. (1997). *Justice interruptus.* New York: Routledge.

Garland, C. (2013). Negating that which negates us. *Radical Philosophy Review, 16*(1), 375–385.

Glenn, E. N. (2015). Settler colonialism as structure: A framework for comparative studies of US race and gender formation. *Sociology of Race and Ethnicity, 1*(1), 52–72.

Goldstein, A. (2008). Where the nation takes place: Proprietary regimes, antistatism, and US settler colonialism. *South Atlantic Quarterly, 107*(4), 833–861.

Gómez-Barris, M. (2012). Mapuche hunger acts: Epistemology of the decolonial. *TRANSMODERNITY: Journal of Peripheral Cultural Production of the Luso-Hispanic World, 1*(3), 120–132.

Gutiérrez y Muhs, G., Niemann, Y. F., González, C. G., & Harris, A. P. (2012). *Presumed incompetent: The intersections of race and class for women in academia.* Boulder, CO: Utah State University Press.

Honneth, A. (1992/1996). *The struggle for recognition: The moral grammar of social conflicts.* Cambridge, MA: MIT Press.

Innes, R. A. (2015). Mohawk interruptus: Life across the borders of settler states by Audra Simpson (review). *Journal of Colonialism and Colonial History, 16*(2). doi:10.1353/cch.2015.0024

Kelley, R. D. (2016). Black study, Black struggle. *The Boston Review.* Retrieved from http://bostonreview.net/forum/robin-d-g-kelley-black-study-black-struggle

Kymlicka, W. (1995). *Multicultural citizenship: A liberal theory of minority rights.* Oxford: Clarendon Press.

Kymlicka, W., & Bashir, B. (2008). *The politics of reconciliation in multicultural societies.* Oxford: Oxford University Press.

Marcuse, H. (2013). (Translation from original, 1964). *One-dimensional man: Studies in the ideology of advanced industrial society.* London: Routledge.

McGranahan, C. (2016). Theorizing refusal: An introduction. *Cultural Anthropology, 31*(3), 319–325. https://culanth.org/articles/817-theorizing-refusal-an-introduction

Mignolo, W. (2011). Epistemic disobedience and the decolonial option: A manifesto. *TRANSMODERNITY: Journal of Peripheral Cultural Production of the Luso-Hispanic World, 1*(2), 44–66.

Moten, F., & Harney, S. (2004). The university and the undercommons: Seven theses. *Social Text, 22*(2), 101–115.

Niemann, Y. F. (2012). Lessons from the experiences of women of color working in academia. In M. G. Gutierrez, Y. F. Niemann, C. G. Gonzalez, & A. P. Harris (Eds.), *Presumed incompetent: The intersections of race and class for women in academia* (pp. 446–499). Boulder, CO: University Press of Colorado.

Povinelli, E. A. (2001). Radical worlds: The anthropology of incommensurability and inconceivability. *Annual Review of Anthropology, 30,* 319–334.

Quijano, A. (1991). Colonialidad y modernidad/racionalidad. Perú Indígena, *29,* 11–21.

Rodríguez, D. (2012). Racial/colonial genocide and the "neoliberal academy": In excess of a problematic. American Quarterly, *64*(4), 809–813.

Simpson, A. (2007). On ethnographic refusal: Indigeneity, 'voice' and colonial citizenship. *Junctures: The Journal for Thematic Dialogue, 9,* 67–80.

Simpson, A. (2014). *Mohawk interruptus: Political life across the borders of settler states.* Durham NC: Duke University Press.

Taylor, C., Gutmann, A., & Taylor, C. (1994). *Multiculturalism: Examining the politics of recognition.* Princeton, NJ: Princeton University Press.

Tuck, E., & Yang, K. W. (2012). Decolonization is not a metaphor. Decolonization: Indigeneity, Education & Society, *1*(1), 1–40.

Undercommoning. (2017). Undercommoning: Revolution within, against, and beyond the university. Retrieved from http://undercommoning.org/undercommoning-within-against-and-beyond/

Wilder, C. S. (2014). *Ebony and ivy: Race, slavery, and the troubled history of America's universities.* New York: Bloomsbury Publishing USA.

Wilderson, F. B. (2003). The prison slave as hegemony's (silent) scandal. *Social Justice, 30*(2), 18–27.

Wilderson III, F. B. (2010). *Red, white & black: Cinema and the structure of US antagonisms.* Durham, NC: Duke University Press.

Wolfe, P. (1999). *Settler colonialism and the transformation of anthropology: The politics and poetics of an ethnographic event.* London: Cassell.

Wolfe, P. (2006). Settler colonialism and the elimination of the native. *Journal of Genocide Research,* 8(4), 387–409.

Wolfe, P. (2013). Recuperating binarism: A heretical introduction. *Settler Colonial Studies, 3*(3–4), 257–279.

4

TOWARD JUSTICE AS ONTOLOGY

Disability and the Question of (In)Difference

Nirmala Erevelles

The question of justice at the intersection of social difference becomes a fraught discussion when disability enters the fray. It is generally assumed that disability is unlike other categories of social difference (such as race, gender, sexuality, and class) because it is thought to embody actual physiological, biological, psychological, and cognitive differences from some mythical social norm, which is itself a social construction (Davis, 1995). Of course, human bodies are all different from each other, but, in popular parlance, the difference that disability embodies is construed as deviant difference. As a result, activists located at these axes of difference have often distanced themselves from the category of disability and the difference it embodies, in their quest to even approach the rather dim prospect of social justice. Thus, one can often hear variations of this familiar refrain from marginalized groups, who, while asserting their value in an unjust world, implicitly and/or explicitly negate disability by claiming that, "we may be black/brown, poor, queer, undocumented, indigenous, migrant, or female, but we are not pathological, not stupid, not crazy, not incapable... in other words, we are not disabled." This refrain, I argue, unwittingly cleaves to an ableist logic rooted in humanist notions of subjectivity that serve as the condition of eligibility in the quest for social justice. To put it simply, then, to even approach the question of justice along the axes of race, class, gender, indigeneity, and sexuality is to just simply refuse to be disabled.

It is for this reason, then, that I am compelled to answer the central question of this edited volume, "Toward what justice?," by articulating a theory of justice that can also account for a radical ontology of disability. I admit that I am making a polemical claim here when I state rather simplistically that the question of justice is actually the question of (a radical) ontology (of disability). To support this claim, I foreground the ways in which discourses of difference have deployed disability rhetorically as an oppressive prosthetic device (Mitchell & Snyder, 2000) even while envisioning just futures at the intersection of social difference. Here, I explore the social, political, and economic implications of such rhetorical articulations of disability as "dead metaphor" (Titchkosky, 2015) for (intersected) disabled subjects whose erasure/eradication often become the very prerequisite for emancipation of the excluded/oppressed Other. Additionally, I subject disability studies scholarship to a critique from the standpoint of race, class, feminism, and queer theory in its own articulation of a vision of social justice. This is because there has been a tendency in disability studies scholarship to presume that the social category of disability is all encompassing and exists outside of and/or perhaps overwhelms any other aspect of difference (i.e. race, gender, sexuality, indigeneity, and class). I, therefore, argue that notwithstanding one's location along the axes of social difference, the ontology of disability (i.e. how one defines what disability is) becomes the central analytic in articulating one's vision of social justice.

To concretize this argument, I draw on three contemporary moments in the quest for social justice: (i) *August 9, 2014*, Ferguson, MO: The Murder of Michael Brown by the State Police; (ii) *March 2014*, Guinea, Liberia, Sierra Leone: The Ebola Outbreak; (iii) *April 2014*, Flint, MI: Lead Poisoning of the City's Drinking Water. Each of these contemporary moments foregrounds the pathologization of disability at the intersection of race, class (Flint), and Empire (the Ebola Outbreak), which has parallels with a similar naturalized pathologization of disability in U.S. public schools that enables ability/smartness/goodness to be deployed as property (Erevelles, 2002; Leonardo & Broderick, 2011) to support the segregation and criminalization of (disabled) students of color at the brutal intersections of difference. I argue that in each of these contemporary moments, disability becomes the central analytic deployed to justify who is or is not a citizen; who can or cannot be separated from the land; and who should or should not be quarantined in U.S. public education (Erevelles, 2011). Thus, in conclusion I argue that any quest "Toward what justice?" would necessitate an ontological theorization of disability that refuses the language of medicalized difference and instead re-imagines crip futurity at the intersections of race, class, gender, nation, indigeneity, migration, and sexuality.

Disability as "Dead Metaphor"

The 2017 installation of Donald Trump as the 45th President of the United States to the chagrin of those citizens committed to liberal/left politics has brought to the fore a stream of pathological labels to describe their anger at the violent policies directed against the most marginalized communities living in the United States. Diagnostic labels such as "mentally unstable," "narcissistic personality disorder," "sociopath," and/or "psychopath" have been assigned to Trump to explain his chaotic, self-centered, dishonest, boastful, and hyper-competitive personality (Morris, 2017). While I am by no means a supporter of the destructive politics/policies of the current President, I, along with many in the disability community and their allies, are troubled by the uncritical deployment of disability-related labels to serve as monikers for the disgust and disillusionment felt by progressive liberals/leftists.

On June 24, 2016, late-night comedy show host Jimmy Kimmel did a parody borrowed from *Willy Wonka's Chocolate Factory* of the "Troompa Loompas" to mock Trump's decision to build a wall along the U.S.–Mexican border. Nearly a year later, this parody morphed into memes poking fun at the parade of White House staffers being led out by the "Oompa Loompas" in satiric response to the slew of firings enacted by the President. While this meme was shared uncritically across social media by many in the progressive left, the laughter sounded hollow for activists in the disability community and their allies. To those non-disabled social justice activists/scholars bemused at this critique, disability activist and thought leader Rebecca Cokley (2017, para 3) explains:

> The Oompa Loompa imagery is offensive to a large percentage of the dwarfism community. They lack agency, they lack an individual identity, they happily work their days away for free for an Average Height man. When Average Height people want to demean Little People, it's one of the "go to" insults.

The fact that Cokley felt compelled to explain these offensive memes to non-disabled social justice activists/scholars, who, otherwise, generally pride themselves on being especially attuned to oppressive representations of difference, foregrounds their inexplicable indifference to ableist structures. Fiona Campbell (2009) defines ableism as:

> a network of beliefs, processes, and practices that produces a particular kind of self and body (the corporeal standard) that is projected as the perfect, species-typical and therefore essential and fully human. Disability then is cast as a diminished state of being human (5).

Campbell's definition thus describes a system of oppression that is rooted in both epistemological and ontological claims to naturalized understandings of what it means to be fully human. As such, ableism enforces "a *constitutional divide* [emphasis in the text] between perfected naturalized humanity and the aberrant, the unthinkable, quasi-human hybrid and therefore non-human" (Campbell, 2009, p. 6). Thus, in the Kimmel skit, the disdain for Trump's unpredictable and damaging decisions regarding the firing of some of his loyal staff was translated into ableist imagery that was projected onto members of the Dwarfism community perceived as less than human.

Further, returning to Cokley's critique of ableist anti-Trump rhetoric, it is troubling to recognize how non-disabled social justice scholars/activists often fail to discern that real material effects arise as a result of such rhetorical representations of disability. For example, British sociologist Tom Shakespeare (2015, para 36–38) writes:

> …[J]okes about the Dwarfs affect the way that the public thinks of people like me…. Despite the differences, I think all restricted-growth people want the same thing: to live in a world where no one is victimised because of their stature.
>
> Research into prejudice in the dwarfism community, carried out by my department, found that three quarters of those surveyed had received unwanted attention or verbal abuse; nearly two thirds had felt unsafe when out; a third had been physically handled by strangers; one in eight had suffered physical violence.
>
> That's why most of us would rather our peers did not dress up as Munchkins or strippograms. The choices they make damage us all.

The violence meted out against disabled people that Shakespeare just described is not limited to the Dwarfism community; it unfortunately extends beyond it. This is because ableist assumptions support the habitual association of disability with diseased and deficient pathology in constant need of amelioration/cure/elimination (Campbell, 2009). Thus, in social justice circles, the inadvertent ontological erasure of disability is naturalized by "transmogrifying disability into a dead metaphor that people use only to diagnose injustice" (Titchkosky, 2015, p. 2) and/or to justify it (injustice). This, then, raises the question, "[H]ow it is that otherwise politically astute and socially aware people and/or movements want and seemingly need impairment rhetoric to drive their social justice endeavors [and/or explain them away]?" (Titchkosky, 2015, p. 2). Moreover, as per Titchkosky's argument, disability is discursively constituted as ontology's negation; hence its transmogrification into a dead metaphor.

Titchkosky (2015) points out that disability as a dead metaphor is also habitually deployed in social justice rhetoric to describe the embodied experience of oppression. Here is a sampling of phrases that she lists:

> color blind, deaf to the call of justice, suffering from historical amnesia; blind to structural oppression, limping under the weight of inequality; an amputated self, simply crazy, subject to colonial aphasia, agnosia, even alexia; nothing but a deformed autonomy made to fit a crippled economy—devastatingly disabled.
>
> *(Titchkosky, 2015, p. 1)*

In each of these examples, disability is once again emptied out of all ontological meaning and left to languish like an empty shell to be inhabited by whatever oppressive epithet is thrown its way. Here, disability serves "as an opportunistic metaphorical device" in discourses of (in)justice, "*a narrative prosthesis*" [emphasis in the text], so to speak, signifying social, political, and economic collapse (Mitchell & Snyder, 2006, p. 205). Mitchell and Snyder (2006) have coined the phrase "narrative prosthesis" to indicate that "disability has been used throughout history as a crutch upon which literary [and social (in)justice] narratives lean for their representation power, disruptive potentiality, and analytical insight" (p. 206). In the Kimmel skit, the Oompa Loompas serve as a prosthetic propelling the narrative of Trump's inadequacies forward, enabling a vision of social justice to exist just outside the abnormalities that disability is seen to embody. Thus, escaping this habitual quagmire in social justice circles requires that we explore "alternative ways of rethinking the abnormal" (Davis, 1995, p. 49) as well as the (un)just that refuse disability as a "dead metaphor."

(White) Disability Studies and the Struggle with Difference

At the same time, within the vast diversity which is the disability community, ontological erasures also prevail. Mainstream disability studies scholarship projects (perhaps inadvertently) the ideal disabled subject of social justice efforts to be the cis gender, white, heteronormative, middle-class, disabled male. Given the rampant ableism that thrives unrecognized in the social sphere, this ideal disabled subject has to contend with inaccessibility in the public sphere, segregation and/or exclusion in educational and employment contexts, poverty and social isolation in residential settings, and the constant threat of involuntary incarceration and abusive care in nursing homes and residential state hospitals (Davis, 2006; Goodley, 2016; Oliver & Barnes, 1998). And yet, even though the material effects of everyday life with a disability are quite devastating for the idealized disabled subject I just described, the vision of justice articulated from this standpoint fails to address the different experiences of injustice faced by disabled people located differentially along the axes of race, gender, sexuality, class, indigencity, and nation.

There have been interventions in disability studies to engage with other categories of difference within the disability community, notably around the politics of gender (Fine & Asch, 1988; Garland-Thomson, 2002; Ghai, 2003; Hall, 2011) and queer theory (Kafer, 2013; McRuer, 2006). For example, Rosemarie Garland-Thomson (2011, p. 17) argues that:

> the informing premise of feminist disability theory is that disability, like femaleness, is not a natural state of corporeal inferiority, inadequacy, excess, or stroke of misfortune... [but] [r]ather a culturally fabricated narrative of the body.

As such, feminist disability studies "provide insight into how thinking critically about disability creates an opening for interrogation of the borders that define feminist theory, philosophy, and other fields of inquiry" (Hall, 2015, p. 1). From a social justice perspective then, a feminist disability studies perspective raises critical questions regarding gendered and ableist conceptions of autonomy, care, and vulnerability; about ableist and gendered notions of "good" and "bad" mothers; about sterilization abuse and custody denial for disabled women; and, last but not least, what it means to "incorporate understandings of the interdependence and vulnerability of the human condition in the development of theories of justice" (Hall, 2015, p. 9).

Just like how feminist disability studies have extended feminist conceptualizations of social justice, disability studies scholars, through "crippin'" queer theory, have also reconceptualized social justice in queer space. "Crippin'," according to Robert McRuer (2006), refers, in part, to critical analytical practices that explore how:

> cultures of ability or disability are conceived, materialized, spatialized, and populated... [within] geographies of uneven development [and] are mapped onto bodies marked by differences of race, class, gender, and ability.
> *(McRuer, 2006, p. 72)*

Thus, in crippin' queer theory, McRuer proposes a *critically queer/severely disabled* identity, that "[resists] the demands for able-bodiedness,...[in order] to work the weakness in the norm" (p. 30). Alison Kafer (2013), in her book, *Feminist Queer Crip*, building on the arguments from feminist disability studies and crip theory, begins to trace some of those queer/crip connections. Kafer's (2013) intervention for the project of social justice is to trace where compulsory able-bodiedness/able-mindedness and compulsory heterosexuality intertwine in the service of normativity in order to:

> examine how terms like "defective," "deviant," and "sick" have been used to justify discrimination against people whose bodies, minds, desires and practices differ from the unmarked norm; to speculate how norms of gendered behavior—proper masculinity and femininity—are based on nondisabled bodies; and to map potential points of connection among, and departure between, queer (and) disability activists.
> *(Kafer, 2013, p. 17)*

Thus, while McRuer and Kafer broaden the scope of disability studies to engage queer/crip connections, it is also possible to recognize how an interrogation into issues of justice from a disability studies perspective moves toward a more radical interrogation of the ontological limits of normativity.

Perhaps one of the most scathing critiques from within disability studies scholarship has come from the critical location of race. In 2006, the late Chris Bell wrote an essay calling out disability studies scholarship for producing what he called "White Disability Studies." Acknowledging that this exclusion was not intentional, Bell pointed out that its inadvertent outcome has been a "tendency to whitewash disability history, ontology, and phenomenology (p. 275)." While Bell was not the first scholar/activist to critically engage with race and disability (Baynton, 2001, 2005; Erevelles, 2002; James & Wu, 2006), he was the first to foreground how whiteness permeated disability studies scholarship and colluded with ableism to render disabled/queer people of color invisible. Since Bell's tongue-in-cheek "modest proposal," the field of disability studies has taken heed and there has been a notable increase in scholarship that engages both race and disability. However, more than a decade after Bell's "modest proposal," there is still a paucity of scholarship that moves beyond an additive framework committed to some variation of the rather simplistic analogy: "Being disabled is just like being black." Thus, moving away from this problematic analogy that fails to envision social justice for those trapped at the intersections of race and disability, I have argued that race and disability are mutually constitutive of each other, and that disability studies scholarship should reflect this intersectional complexity (Erevelles, 2011).

More recently, Annamma, Connor, and Ferri (2012) have named this intersectional perspective "Dis/ability Critical Race Studies" or "DisCrit." According to Annamma et al. (2012), DisCrit rejects the habitual practice of simply adding disability to analyses of the intersectional politics of race, class, gender identity, and sexuality to argue that "racism and ableism are normalizing processes that are interconnected and collusive" (p. 7). Grounding their argument specifically in educational contexts (but not limited to these contexts), Annamma et al. (2012, p. 15) describe how:

> dis/ability and race first became equated and molded through pseudo-sciences, but [were] later further cemented through seemingly 'objective' clinical assessment practices... [that were then] reified through laws, policies, and programs until these concepts became uncritically conflated and viewed as the natural order of things.

Nestled in the interplay of these discursive and material practices are the politics of citizenship that bring race and disability into play by:

> triggering stereotypic associations with weaknesses, including fears of individuals seen as unhealthy, unable to adequately compete in work and war, with their reproductive potential questioned, feared or even forcibly managed.
>
> *(Annamma et al., 2012, p. 16)*

As such, DisCrit foregrounds the problematic ways in which the (non) recognition of racialized bodies as citizens is materialized via the oppressive practices of, for example, educational segregation, immigration policies, and incarceration, by associating racialized bodies with discourses of disability that are the apparent embodiment of degeneracy and dis/respectability.

In this section I have argued that disability is invoked both discursively and materially in practices of (in)justice at the intersection of social difference. Unfortunately, non-disabled social justice scholars/activists fail to recognize this centrality and instead deploy disability as a prosthetic device to either explain and/ or embody injustice. It is in this context, then, that Titchkosky (2015, p. 6) calls on scholars/activists to carefully attend to this:

> 'paradox of reference' within the historical imbrications of race, gender, and disability where these terms may repeat the tragedies from which they spring even as we try to re-make colonial history. Given the welter of impairment references in social justice praxis, this paradox of reference invites a consideration of how "disability studies" itself has grown from this colonial history.

This "paradox of reference" that Titchkosky refers to speaks to this doubling up of disability rhetoric in social justice work—where disability is constituted at the site of oppression even while it enables us to reconstitute those very sites in the cause for social justice. Thus, in the remaining sections of this chapter, I will describe three contemporary moments where this "paradox of reference" is materialized so as to map out spaces of possibility for radical intersectional work toward social justice.

August 9, 2014, Ferguson, MO: The Police Murder of Michael Brown

One hot, August afternoon, Michael Brown, an unarmed, young, Black, soon-to-be college freshman was shot by a police officer; his body left on the hot blacktop for many hours, carelessly quarantined from his community who gathered on the sidewalk both tearful and angry. The lax yellow police tape separating the slowly gathering crowd on the grassy roadside seemed ineffectual to contain the soon-to-be outrage that would spark a movement—Black Lives Matter—that would also propel a little-known small Missouri town into national and international prominence. By nightfall, the unearthly silence that marked the scene of the murder would be replaced by the whine of bullets, the crackle of tear gas, the sirens, the shattering of glass, and screams of pain amidst fire and smoke and blood, and a mounting, desperate rage. The state police, intent on protecting private property belligerently faced off against a mass of Brown, Black, and (several) white bodies with hands raised up to say, "Don't shoot!" But it must not matter… because the police shootings continue unabated as more bodies fall—almost all of them Brown and Black, many of them disabled. Here is a solemn roll call:

> In Memoriam Darien Hunt, Ezell Ford, Omar Abrego, Tamir Rice, Tanesha Anderson, Rumai Brisbon, John Crawford III, Keith Vidal, Kajieme Powell, Akai Gurley, Eric Garner, Michelle Cusseaux, Jack Jacquez, Jason Harrison,

Yvette Smith, Louis Rodriguez, Matthew Pollow, Dontre Hamilton, David Latham, Maria Godinez, Deshwanda Sanchez, Michelle Vash Payne, Ty Underwood, Lamia Beard among so many others whose deaths we do not know of and hence remain unmournable.

So, are the almost daily murders of Brown/Black/disabled/queer/transgender bodies a recent "epidemic" or are such murders "endemic" to U.S. society given its brutal history of settler colonialism, slavery, imperialism, religious fundamentalism, and transnational capitalism? I use the terms "epidemic" and "endemic" tentatively—conscious that I am drawing on medical terms to talk about social, political, and economic phenomena. While an "epidemic" is described as rapidly spreading between bodies in a short period of time (Oxford English Dictionary, n.d.), the term "endemic" refers to disease that is chronically prevalent in a specific context and region and is sometimes assumed to be native/natural to the region (Oxford English Dictionary, n.d.). Following this logic, while an "epidemic" can be halted in its tracks through concerted efforts to eradicate it, a disease that is "endemic" is assumed to be stubbornly resistant to any/all interventions. Given these definitions, what are the implications of reading these murders through these two radically different lenses?

The problem with the terms "epidemic" and "endemic" is that they are usually deployed via nation-state/transnational practices to mark some bodies as pathological and therefore dangerous to other bodies. As a result, to stem an epidemic of some bodies construed as "endemically" pathological from invading/assailing/infecting (white) normative space, the nation-state enables practices of eradication/destruction (e.g. murder via state violence; sterilization; euthanasia) and/or quarantine/containment (e.g. imprisonment, institutionalization; school segregation; special education). In fact, quarantine and destruction are nation-state/transnational practices whose justification lies in the pathologization of the ontological conceptualizations located at the intersection of race and disability. Thus, while I am uncomfortable about invoking these medical terms from a critical disability studies perspective, in this context I flip the racist and ableist script in order to foreground the historical structures and material conditions that enable this "epidemic of violence" that appears "endemic" to nation-state/transnational practices of eradication and/or quarantine to prevail.

One immediate response to this "epidemic of violence" has been one of pathologizing the victims. Here, race and disability are implicated simultaneously as both the cause and outcome of "epidemic violence." For example, the death of Eric Garner, the Staten Island African-American man who died after the police placed him in a chokehold, was blamed on his obesity, asthma, and heart disease, instead of on the excessive force used by the police. Interestingly enough, regarding death by chokeholds, McRuer (2006), in his book *Crip Theory*, mentions in passing that the LAPD justified the deaths of gang members of the Crips and Bloods at the hands of the police by claiming that the carotid chokehold when placed on African-Americans did not open up as fast as they do on "normal" [sic] people.

In both examples described above, disability as pathology is used to justify state violence against its Black citizens. Here, the intent of a pathological intervention is the single-minded decision to destroy the isolated contravening agent assumed to have been the cause of the epidemic in the first place. Thus, since the victims of these epidemics are perceived as the very embodiment of pathological difference, they become the objects of destruction rather than the subjects of care. Claiming that their pathologized bodies locate them outside the boundaries of humanness, the violence that is done to them is justified because they are seen as the state of exception existing within the zone of bare life. Thus, the pathologization of Michael Brown as a dangerous thug not only contributed to his brutal murder in front of witnesses in broad daylight, but also allowed his broken body to lie carelessly on the hot tarmac untended for more than four hours, consigned to what Achilles Mbembe has described as "death worlds." Here it is possible to see how disability and race coalesce to mutually constitute a deadly ontology that prescribes death for Black/Brown bodies and destruction for Black/Brown bodies whether living or dead.

March 2014, Guinea, Liberia, Sierra Leone: The Ebola Outbreak

The early spring of 2014 brought with it its own violent medical epidemic—the spread of the Ebola virus, a severe hemorrhagic fever with a fatality rate ranging from 25% to 90% in humans, according to a World Health Organization report (2014). The same report states that the virus is assumed to be transmitted to people through contact with the blood, secretions, organs, or other bodily fluids of infected animals like chimpanzees, gorillas, fruit bats, monkeys, forest antelope, and porcupines found ill or dead or in the rainforest. The virus then rapidly spreads in the human population through human-to-human transmission. Assumed to have begun its deadly journey through human populations in the African nation of Guinea, the virus spread across land borders to neighboring Sierra Leone and Liberia, by air (one traveler only) to Nigeria, and by land (one traveler) to Senegal. Because these small nation-states already wracked by civil wars also support weak health systems, lacking human and infrastructural resources, efforts to stem the deadly march of the epidemic through impoverished populations has been almost insignificant.

On February 10, 2015, the Center for Disease Control (CDC) reported about 22,999 suspected cases in Guinea, Sierra Leone, and Liberia, and 9,253 deaths. Other nations that have reported cases are Nigeria (20), Mali (eight), the United States (four), UK (one), Spain (one), and Senegal (one). While early supportive care with rehydration and symptomatic treatment improves survival, there have been no licensed treatments, although certain therapies under development were used for a couple of U.S. citizens who survived the deadly illness. Yet given the death toll, Ebola remains a deadly, violent epidemic that has motivated some problematic modes of surveillance, incarceration, and discrimination against those suspected of being carriers of the virus.

In each of these contexts, the immediate response has been one of pathologizing those who have been the victims of these epidemic outbreaks. Here, race and disability are implicated simultaneously as both the cause and outcome of epidemic violence. Similar to the case of Eric Garner, instead of garnering medical and other resources that are desperately needed in the African countries battling Ebola, Africans exposed to the Ebola virus were simultaneously blamed for inadequate health knowledges and backward social practices (disability) for contracting the virus. Moreover, if the victims of any of these epidemics survived the violence, they were bound to acquire disabilities as a result of inadequate care and other untreated side effects.

Scholars in both critical race theory and disability studies know well the dangers of pathologizing bodies. Since pathology is closely associated with the medical model, the emphasis is on cure rather than care. Here the intent of a pathological intervention is the single-minded decision to destroy the isolated contravening agent assumed to have been the cause of the epidemic in the first place. As a result, since the victims of these epidemics are perceived as the very embodiment of pathological difference, they become the objects of destruction rather than the subjects of care. Claiming that their pathologized bodies locate them outside the boundaries of humanness, the violence that is done to them is justified because they are seen as the state of exception existing within the zone of bare life. Thus, the pathologization of Michael Brown as a dangerous thug not only contributed to his brutal murder in front of witnesses in broad daylight, but also allowed his broken body to lie carelessly on the hot tarmac untended for more than four hours. Similarly, the disinterested global response to the Ebola epidemic in countries in Sub-Saharan Africa until it threatened the countries in the Global North was also justified based on the pathologization of African People as the "living dead" via the deployment of a necropolitics that casually consigned their pathologized bodies to what Achilles Mbembe (2006) has described as "death worlds."

April 24, 2014, Flint, MI: Lead Poisoning of the City's Drinking Water

The first time I heard of Flint, Michigan, was when I was watching Michael Moore's 1989 documentary, *Roger and Me*. At that time, witnessing how General Motors (GM) had leeched almost all the life from that city, taking away employment and with it hope, and leaving behind the rusty detritus of closed factories and degraded natural resources, I could not imagine anything worse happening to this already desolate city. And then the news broke... that the water in Flint, Michigan, contained lead so beyond even the limits of dangerous—the water the shade of a dirty gold giving even the double layers of plastic that encased it a poisonous hue. Though the news broke in January 2016, this horribly dangerous crisis was long in "becoming" what it now is—beginning as early as April 24, 2014, when the City of Flint decided to save money by opting to use water from the Flint River (a river already polluted by GM several years earlier) rather than from the Detroit City Water System (*New York Times*, January 21, 2016). Almost immediately, residents complained of its taste and its odor, witnessed their bodies erupt in boils and rashes, seemingly in protest against the toxic bacteria found there, and demanded action, only to be told that they needed to boil this water several times and to calm down. There was no palpable threat.

It is this threat of what exists in this water supply that is critical to our questions about disability and race and class. Whose bodies were presumed to be immune to this threat? Remember, this threat began almost at the same time as the global terror over the Ebola virus in West Africa. What does it mean that the Center of Disease Control (CDC) and the Environmental Protection Agency (EPA) and the Department of Homeland Security (DHS) were not desperate to destroy/isolate/quarantine this vector of disease and eradicate its deadly spread through its most desolate citizenry? Is it because, in this case, the pathologies of destruction lie not in bodies but in the political and economic histories contaminating the very infrastructures that are central to the nourishment of our bodies, our lives? How does this realization decompose the very notion of citizenship (the right to life, liberty, and the pursuit of happiness, and its corresponding responsibilities) in the context of such egregious acts of environmental (in)justice and its potent threat to the citizenry in the so-called First World country in the Global North?

More importantly, what exactly is this threat and what does it do to the possibility of imagining critical coalitions around disability and its associated categories of difference? We know that even the smallest presence of lead in the bloodstream can cause impairments, both physical and cognitive. What does this recognition signify to our burgeoning radical disability community? How does Disability Pride jostle for recognition in the hostile ableist context where disability is commonly thought of as social death? And what will this proliferation of disabled bodies do to the disability movement when these bodies located at the intersections of race, class, disability, queer identities belong nowhere and are claimed by no one—perhaps because a callous political economy seems to overwhelm the sense of cultural collectivity when disability makes itself known in each of these diverse groups (remember, minority groups have had to claim that they are not disabled in order to be recognized).

The fact, though, that ableism constructs disability as "social death" is concretely materialized via the effects of lead poisoning that bring impairments found in children of color living in low-income neighborhoods. La Paperson (2010) has called these spaces of desolation "the postcolonial ghetto"—an urban space of dislocation. In another characterization, Richard Sennett (1996) has described this sequestering of unwanted racialized and classed bodies as "an urban condom"—protecting urban residents from the polluting intercourse of its outcasts. Note again that these representations focus on who is pathologized in these representations as well as what conditions/spaces/events produce such pathologization. Because lead poisoning can create both cognitive and behavioral impairments, many of these children are consigned to the segregated, under-resourced, punitive educational contexts of special education that eventually become, for several of these children, a fast track along the school-to-prison pipeline. Valerie Polakow (2000) described these conditions as social toxicity.

Thus, if we shift from the policed streets into our policed schools, we see yet another example of how the nation-state practice of quarantine work are utilized to once again consign disabled students living at the intersections of race/gender/class to the "death worlds" in our schools. In fact, the very logic of schooling is based on disability as a "dead metaphor" and most racialized/gendered and queer others have sought to distance themselves from disability. Educational contexts treat disability as a medical/physiological deficit and disabled students as pathologically misfit rather than recognizing disability as a social and political category. In fact, the very logic of neoliberal capitalist education can only perceive disability as a drain to its profit-seeking aims. As a result, the gulags of special education/alternative schooling and the school-to-prison pipeline proliferate in educational contexts—quarantine spaces accepted as the most normative aspect of schooling because disability as a "dead metaphor" is seldom deconstructed even within radical pedagogical spaces.

Conclusion

So then, in answer to the question, "Toward what justice?," I return to my earlier argument that the question of justice is really the question of (a radical) ontology (of disability). Refusing the perpetuation of disability as "dead metaphor," Kafer (2013) calls feminist/queer/environmental theorists/activists to account for the ableism that is inadvertently or deliberately intertwined in their transgressive/oppositional visions for a future that explicitly (or implicitly) excludes the possibility of disability and comes at a huge cost to the disability community. She therefore thoughtfully asks: What does it mean to choose futures for disability? Kafer's question has been answered by legions of disability activists/scholars in Disability Pride parades, in vibrant disability justice movements, in the transgressive aesthetics of disability art, in the angry protests against the medical industrial complex, against incarceration in both prisons and institutions, against sterilization, against segregation in education, against nursing homes, and, more recently, in the newly expanding scholarship and protests against neoliberal doctrines that are anathema to any claims for crip futurity.

But these reformulations of a crip futurity happen at a considerable distance from other social movements where, as Rachel Gorman (2013) points out, such movements reconstitute the disabled subject as white subject, creating a disability rights consciousness that Gorman calls "a kind of disability nationalism" (p. 272), similar to Jasbir Puar's (2013) critique of homonationalism in the context of the problematic racialization of queer politics. In this context then, what allegiances do disabled people located at the crossroads of shifting identities have with a largely white middle/upper-class disability rights movement in the Global North? And how would our contradictions in the face of these real struggles enable us to imagine futures that do not rely on the exploitation and colonization of others?

On the other hand, the tendency of non-disabled people when accosted with disability is to imagine a socially just future that demands "cure" via dis-location/ quarantine and/or eradication/death. In fact, these are the normative practices of "neoliberal ableism" implicated in the violence of Empire and its aftermath. Roland Coloma (2013) defines Empire as not just a geopolitical entity but also as an enactment of power in conjunction with colonialism, neocolonialism, and imperialism. What Coloma fails to note, and what is central to the functioning of Empire, is the proliferation/production of disability that maps out transnational histories that spill over and seep across national borders and through racialized bodies marked by casual acts of violence justified by ideologies that are simultane-ously ableist and racist.

For example, I call upon all of us to witness the brutality that barricades citizens behind the rubble in the West Bank and the Gaza Strip mediated by the tense rela-tionships between Palestinian territories and Israeli settlements. Moreover, these normalized sites of violence—also known formally as "national borders"—enact practices of "cure" with disability as a natural/normal outcome of such violence. A similar argument could be made when describing the U.S. Mexican Border, where unaccompanied immigrant children without documentation are herded out of immigration detention centers where they had earlier been warehoused (quarantined) for deportation even while being subject to unimaginable physical and emotional stresses—another example of disability proliferation at the inter-section of race, nation, imperialism, exploitative labor, antagonistic class relations, and profit. Here, once again, notions of "cure" are deployed to justify involuntary incarceration that is not limited to the locale of prisons, asylums, nursing homes, and institutions but should also include immigration detention centers, border control policies, and settler colonial land appropriation that are connected to the violent political economy of globalization that enables capital to cross borders with impunity but not racialized labor. In these contexts, the pursuit of "cure" and the practice of "quarantine" result in not just a gross denial of one's human rights as global citizens; rather, these practices also become an instrument of physical harm, disappearance, and even death.

In their essay "Decolonization is not a metaphor" (2012), Eve Tuck and K. Wayne Yang argue that settler colonialism is rooted in a material violence that exceeds affect. They write:

> many Indigenous peoples have been forcibly removed from their homelands onto reservations, indentured, and abducted into state custody, signaling the form of colonization as simultaneously internal (via boarding schools and

other biopolitical modes of control) and external (via uranium mining on Indigenous land in the U.S. Southwest and oil extraction on Indigenous land in Alaska) with a frontier (the U.S. military still nicknames all enemy territory "Indian Country").

(*Tuck & Wayne Yang, 2012, p. 288*)

Citing Dennis Childs, they argue that "the slave ship and the plantation" and not Bentham's panopticon as presented by Foucault, "operated as spatial, racial, and economic templates for subsequent models of coerced labor and human warehousing—as America's original prison industrial complex" (p. 288). Refusing the facile embrace of decolonization as metaphor, Tuck and Yang call for a rejection of all premature attempts at reconciliation. Instead, their demand is simple. Decolonization specifically requires the repatriation of Indigenous land. To that I would add that it also requires an end to oppressive and exploitative class relations that legitimize these epidemics of violence/violent epidemics that I have described in this chapter.

So then, again, in answer to the question, "Toward what justice?," I would argue that it would depend on how one articulates a radical ontology of disability. This would quite simply mean that justice yearns for recognition of one's humanity—of being mournable. In claiming this, it seems like I am articulating a bleak and desperate form of justice—that seems to claim a recognition in death that it could not attain in life. Perhaps what is even brutally poignant is the reality that these pathologized bodies are treated as contagions to be destroyed even after death. Thus, for example, the pathologization of Michael Brown and Eric Garner actually continued with greater "scientific" force after their murders. In fact, in both cases, the destruction of their bodies (and by necessity their personhood) by medicalized discourse that continued after their deaths, rendered them un-mournable and thus outside certain visions of justice at the intersections of race and disability.

But I also see justice as having a hopeful future. I see the quest for social justice in enabling us to stop for a moment and ponder ways in which we can weave our struggles together into an oppositional tapestry whose goal is not inclusion (too liberal and problematic) but rather transformative in collective and complex ways. How do we hold each other and ourselves accountable for transformative praxis within and across differences? In doing so, how do we maintain both specificity and generality as we move between the local and global? In honor of all those whose lives have been lost and/or dis-located, I call on us all to actively work toward crip futurities across borders… beyond metaphor… beyond affect… beyond innocence and toward an intersectional justice that envisions a radical crip futurity for all of us.

Works Referenced

Annamma, S., Connor, D., & Ferri, B. (2013). Dis/ability critical race studies (DisCrit): Theorizing at the intersections of race and dis/ability. *Race Ethnicity and Education*, *16*(1), 1–31.

Baynton, D. (2001). Disability and the justification of inequality in American history. In P. Longmore and L. Umansky (Eds.), *The new disability history: American perspectives* (pp. 33–57). New York: New York University Press.

Baynton, D. (2005). Slaves, immigrants, and suffragists: The uses of disability in citizenship debates. *PMLA, 120*(2), 562–567.

Bell, C. (2006). Introducing white disability studies: A modest proposal. In L. Davis (Ed.), *The Disability Studies Reader* (2nd ed.; pp. 275–282). New York, NY: Taylor and Francis.

Campbell, F. (2009). *Contours of ableism: The production of disability and abledness.* New York: Springer.

Cokley, R. (2017, July 22). Not your Oompa Loompa. Politics means politics. Retrieved from https://politicsmeanspolitics.com/not-your-oompa-loompa-852224777847

Coloma, R. S. (2013). Empire: An analytical category for educational research. *Educational Theory, 63*(6), 639–658.

Davis, L. J. (1995). *Enforcing normalcy: Disability, deafness, and the body.* New York: Verso.

Davis, L. J. (Ed.). (2006). *The disability studies reader* (2nd ed.). New York: Taylor & Francis.

Erevelles, N. (2002). Cognitive disability, race, and the politics of citizenship. *Disability, Culture and Education, 1*(1), 5–25.

Erevelles, N. (2011). *Disability and difference in global contexts: Enabling a transformative body politic.* New York: Springer.

Fine, M., & Asch, A. (1988). Disability beyond stigma: Social interaction, discrimination, and activism. *Journal of Social Issues, 44*(1), 3–21.

Garland-Thomson, R. (2002). Integrating disability, transforming feminist theory. *NWSA Journal, 14*(3), 1–32.

Garland-Thomson, R. (2011). Misfits: A feminist materialist disability concept. *Hypatia, 26*(3), 591–609.

Ghai, A. (2003). *(Dis)embodied form: Issues of disabled women.* Delhi, India: Har-Anand Publications.

Goodley, D. (2016). *Disability studies: An interdisciplinary introduction.* New York: Sage.

Gorman, R. (2013). Mad nation? Thinking through race, class, and mad identity politics. In B. A. LeFrançois, R. Menzies, & G. Reaume (Eds.), *Mad matters: A critical reader in Canadian mad studies* (pp. 269–280). Toronto: Canadian Scholars' Press.

Hall, K. Q. (Ed.). (2011). *Feminist disability studies.* Bloomington, IN: Indiana University Press.

Hall, K. Q. (2015). New conversations in feminist disability studies: Feminism, philosophy, and borders. *Hypatia, 30*(1), 1–12.

James, J. C., & Wu, C. (2006). Editors' introduction: Race, ethnicity, disability, and literature: Intersections and interventions. *Melus, 31*(3), 3–13.

Kafer, A. (2013). *Feminist, queer, crip.* Bloomington, IN: Indiana University Press.

La Paperson (2010). The postcolonial ghetto: Seeing her shape and his hand. *Berkeley Review of Education, 1*(1). Retrieved from https://escholarship.org/uc/item/3q91f9gv

Leonardo, Z., & Broderick, A. (2011). Smartness as property: A critical exploration of intersections between whiteness and disability studies. *Teachers College Record, 113*(10), 2206–2232.

Mbembe, A. (2006). Necropolitics. *Raisons politiques, 1,* 29–60.

McRuer, R. (2006). *Crip theory: Cultural signs of queerness and disability.* New York: New York University Press.

Mitchell, D. T., & Snyder, S. L. (2000). *Narrative prosthesis: Disability and the dependencies of discourse.* Ann Arbor, MI: University of Michigan Press.

Mitchell, D., & Snyder, S. (2006). The materiality of metaphor. In L. Davis (Ed.), *The disability studies reader* (2nd ed.; pp. 205–216). New York: Taylor & Francis.

Moore, M. (Producer & Director). (1989). *Roger and Me*. USA: Dog Eat Dog Productions.

Morris, A. (2017, April 7). Why Trump is not mentally fit to be President. *Rolling Stone*. Retrieved from www.rollingstone.com/politics/features/trump-and-the-pathology-of-narcissism-w474896

The New York Times Magazine (2016, January 21). Events that led to the Flint Water Crisis. Retrieved from www.nytimes.com/interactive/2016/01/21/us/flint-lead-water-timeline.html

Oliver, M., & Barnes, C. (1998). *Disabled people and social policy: From exclusion to inclusion*. London: Addison Wesley Longman.

Oxford English Dictionary (n.d.) Endemic. Retrieved from https://en.oxforddictionaries.com/definition/endemic

Oxford English Dictionary (n.d.) Epidemic. Retrieved from https://en.oxforddictionaries.com/definition/epidemic

Polakow, V. (Ed.). (2000). *The public assault on America's children: Poverty, violence, and juvenile injustice* (Vol. 5). New York: Teachers College Press.

Puar, J. (2013). Rethinking homonationalism. *International Journal of Middle East Studies, 45*(2), 336–339.

Sennett, R. (1996). Flesh and stone: The body and the city in Western civilization. New York: WW Norton & Company.

Shakespeare, T. (2015, February 6) 'It's time dwarfs stopped demeaning themselves in public'. *The Telegraph*. Retrieved from www.telegraph.co.uk/culture/tvandradio/11394321/Its-time-dwarfs-stopped-demeaning-themselves-in-public.html

Titchkosky, T. (2015). Life with dead metaphors: Impairment rhetoric in social justice praxis. *Journal of Literary & Cultural Disability Studies, 9*(1), 1–18.

Tuck, E., & Yang, K. W. (2012). Decolonization is not a metaphor. *Decolonization: Indigeneity, Education & Society*, 1(1).

World Health Organization. (2014). *WHO: Ebola response roadmap situation report 24 December 2014*. Retrieved from http://apps.who.int/iris/bitstream/10665/146311/1/roadmapsitrep_24Dec14_eng.pdf?ua=1

5

AGAINST SOCIAL JUSTICE AND THE LIMITS OF DIVERSITY

Or Black People and Freedom

Rinaldo Walcott

In Memory of Andrew Loku
(murdered by Toronto Police Services on July 5, 2015)

The staving fellah (or the jobless inner city N.H.I., the global New Poor or les damnes), Fanon pointed out, does not have to inquire into the truth. He is, they are the Truth. It is we who institute this "Truth". We must now undo their narratively condemned status.
(Sylvia Wynter, "No Humans Involved: An Open Letter to My Colleagues")

I have nothing soothing to tell you
that's not my job,
my job is to revise and revise this bristling list,
hourly.

(Dionne Brand, Inventory)

On November 4, 2015, Prime Minister Justin Trudeau announced what was quickly hailed as the most diverse Canadian cabinet ever. When asked about his diverse cabinet and particularly its gender parity, PM Trudeau quipped, "because it is 2015" (The Canadian Press, 2015). Yet, as quickly as the claim of "most diverse" was uttered, it was also criticized. On both social media and in the mainstream media, a debate emerged about what constitutes diversity, and further, what constitutes representation. This debate pointed to the limits of gender parity as diversity, when race and ethnicity also enter the frame. The debate delimited the phenotypic features of PM Trudeau's cabinet, pointing to Indigenous women, South Asian, and Middle Eastern Members of Parliament (MPs) as a way to get beyond the limit of gender parity as diversity. Through all of this chatter, glaringly absent from the phenotypic cohort were Black MPs.

In this chapter, I tangle with the idea that the language of people of color (POC) and diversity is an obscuring language. By this I mean that logics of POC and diversity, or as is often used in the academic context, "race," lacks specificity and therefore cannot continue to do the necessary work of destroying antiblackness. The invocation of diversity is meant to suggest that the work of "race," of equity, is being done and that representation is being worked. However, such assumptions can obscure exactly who is being included and represented, as is made clear in the composition of PM Trudeau's cabinet. As Michi Saagiig Nishnaabeg writer, musician, and scholar Leanne Simpson pointed out on Twitter, how does one celebrate Indigenous "inclusion" while not noticing antiblackness and Black exclusion? This question posed by Simpson is but one way of getting at the way that celebrations of inclusion can mask Black exclusion, while sidelining critiques of it.

Part 1: Performing Inclusion, or Antiblackness as Institutional Practice

The term "diversity" has a history, of course, but I will attend specifically to its more recent history. In the late 1980s and early 1990s, Black communities in Canada had abandoned the language and logic of diversity as a failed model for inclusion. The refusal of the frame of diversity was premised on the failures of multicultural policies, employment equity policies, and ongoing struggles around policing, education, and children in care. It was in that moment that the language of anti-racism was most forcefully developed and deployed. Here I think of Enid Lee's 1985 book *Letters to Marcia: A Teacher's Guide to Anti-racist Education.* I think of the Black Action Defence Committee's leadership around policing, and the rise of radical Black social workers, community workers, service organizations, and providers. Here I think of how Black women took over publishing houses and open presses, started magazines, and so on. A still unwritten history; one that we can learn much from.

Indeed, by 1990, Black activists and POCs had moved on from the language of diversity to articulate an anti-racism politics that was firmly a structural critique. Considering this history alongside the contemporary widespread taking-up of the term diversity in universities, I have to wonder how it came to be that diversity has again become something in which Black people desire to take part. Recalling the immensely critical rejection of diversity by Black communities in the late 1980s and 1990s, it is somewhat shocking to see the return of the language of diversity as the framing device for measuring what accountability and inclusion might look like for Black people in this geopolitical space called Canada.

In 2015, shortly after Prime Minister Trudeau announced his cabinet, Cecil Foster penned an opinion piece in *The Globe and Mail* titled "Canada's blacks: Still waiting for their moment of 'real change,'" arguing that Black Canadians had been left behind by the son of the father of multiculturalism. Foster wrote:

> But something is missing from this cabinet, from this reflection of the Canada of 2015. There are no people that look like me or my children or my grandchildren, despite there being at least six Liberal caucus members with Caribbean and African immigrant backgrounds. Once again, blacks and blackness are invisible.

Foster's critique is more a lament than a call for a refusal of diversity altogether, and it is executed faithfully to the doctrine of liberal multicultural ethos that would require us to believe that Black representivity is possible. I take the opposite view: that Black representivity is impossible to achieve in our current social, political, and cultural structure. Nonetheless, it is my view that Foster's article exemplified the paradox of Black life in Canada: at once invisible and hypervisible. By this I mean that Foster takes up important representative space in a national newspaper, thereby confirming for some that Blackness is indeed noted, but ironically to pen its invisibility. Whether we are speaking of crime, prisons, joblessness, or education, blackness in Canada occupies a significantly visible role, usually one of the "problem." Blackness simultaneously inhabits an invisible role, a lack of specificity of what the conditions and measures of improvement might be. It is the latter I mark as institutional disregard. By this I mean that there is not a single institution in this nation that takes as foundational that Black people are a necessary element of that which we might make a more hopeful future.

We are in a strange kind of social, political, and cultural settlement in contemporary Canada as far as Black people are concerned. In this chapter, I will not be able to address all the ways in which this settlement is manifested, but I hope that by turning to the site of the cultural as a broader frame of living Black lives, the present state of Canadian engagements with blackness in this historical moment might be paid witness to. In this discussion I am going to make as many broad strokes as possible, to point to very specific instances of antiblackness in Canada. Everywhere we look, Black life is in dire straits in Canada. Along with Indigenous peoples, Black life is stuck somewhere at the bottom of every marker, whether looking at poverty, prisons, joblessness, underemployment, unemployment, housing, or education. What is particularly striking is that no level of government or any other major institution in this nation seems to find it necessary to speak directly to Black people about their collective well-being. Indeed, if any one single thing characterizes contemporary Black life in Canada, it is the way in which Black lives seem not to matter at all, especially in the nation's major institutions—museums, art galleries, universities, government and so on. If there ever was a time that making such a claim could have been rebuked as entirely cynical or even wrong, that time has now passed.

The Veils of Diversity and Compensatory Individualism

Some years ago, I was in a conversation with one of Ontario's Deans of Education. The Dean was very excited by a newly issued report by Roy McMurtry and Alvin Curling, Volume 1 of *The Review of the Roots of Youth Violence* (2008). The report investigated violence among youth, of which Black and Indigenous youth were a significant demographic. The report made addressing mental health issues a major aspect of their recommendations, as they should be. The Dean's excitement, however, was focused on the report's mental health-related recommendations, almost to the exclusion of the other issues and recommendations raised by the report. I wasn't at all surprised. Of course, a Dean of Education would be excited to see the highlighting of mental health (at perhaps the expense of other issues) as being an opportunity. It should be said that *The Review of the Roots of Youth Violence* is also critical of the ways in which public school education still silences Black histories and the ways in which Black histories remain absent from the broader Canadian national imaginary, all issues that a Faculty of Education could and should lead on. Instead, the Dean was more interested in seizing upon the mental health issues and related recommendations, because this was a way to finally access (then) sizable dollars of Canadian Institutes of Health Research (CIHR). The then-sizable grants from CIHR would make any Dean swoon in the context of tight university budgets. The Dean could have imagined a range of ways to use the report's recommendations to bring more critical forms of diversity, and in particular Black scholarship, to her faculty, but she could not go there.

This is one small example that leads to my claim that the Canadian academy is structurally antiblack and only interested in Black people in so far as it furnishes the agendas and priorities of those who are already there; that is, those who are already inside the structure—those who are marked white. The overall Canadian academy has failed similarly; its inability to imagine blackness and Black peoples beyond small compensatory acts is evident everywhere. What work are universities doing to bring forms of critical diversity to our workplace? What role are universities taking to provide space for the non-white Canadians, especially the Black emerging scholars that I train? At the local levels of our faculties and departments, how are we creating the terms under which these knowledges might enter our institution, especially Black knowledges? Interestingly, I can answer these questions quite easily. Nothing is being done, and this is despite many good policies put in place that are meant to activate such actions and outcomes.

Over a decade ago, I served as the Affirmative Action Director at York University. That position gave me crucial insight into the ways in which Canadian academics work hard to keep things as they are. Most recently, I served as an advisor on diversity and accessibility at Ontario Institute for Studies in Education at the University of Toronto. The experience was the same. The performative non-performativity of reproducing whiteness is skilled at writing policy and negligent at implementing it, all the while making claims to being committed to doing otherwise.

In the Canadian academic context, all of our claims of diversity, anti-racism, equity, and social justice are institutional performative non-performativity in service of the status quo. As a Black studies scholar who entered the Canadian academic job market in 1995, I can say that the university's demographic constitution has not changed much over that 21-year period of my tenure. In short, from my vantage point, it has been more that 20 years of the same view for Black scholars in this country. In this time period, I have witnessed how contraband Black knowledges have been smuggled into the university under the guise of race studies, ethnic studies, multicultural studies, and anti-racism. In each instance, the specificity of Black life is disappeared as Black scholars are asked to do more than Black studies. Black studies is positioned as never sufficient, unlike other fields. What is particularly daunting is that in areas such as cultural studies, Canadian studies, and women and gender studies—areas that one might want to believe hold a different, and dare I say, more critical relationship to their institutionality—the same antiblack practices are at work. Ethically, the stakes are higher for those areas of study as "intellectual practice[s] of politics" as Stuart Hall (1992, p. 285) names it, to begin to shift the overwhelming white Canadian academy, to at least begin the tasks of resembling the demographics of the nation-formation, especially in the urban areas where most of us now live.

Antiblackness is Inlaid in "Diversity"

I understand antiblackness as a structure and a set of practices, practices that are fundamentally conditioned to offer blackness no way in. These conditions are not always explicit; rather, they are the philosophical foundation that structures the inevitability of antiblack illegibility. With such in mind, attempts to fix existing structures can only but result in failure, because the structure itself is built on logics and practices meant to offer blackness no space within. I am influenced by the work of Frank B. Wilderson (2010) as well as Tamara Nopper (2011), who draws on Wilderson to point to the "void of non-relation" that conditions others' non-relationship to Black peoples. The Black subject, then, has no relation to others in Western traditions which, since Enlightenment, have been founded on the production of the Black subject as a thing. Indeed, reckoning with antiblackness, or afro-pessimism, as my friends and colleagues call that reckoning, is such that one might walk away feeling that all forms of resistance are impossible and futile. The afro-pessimism of Black scholars and thinkers wants us to recognize that because the structure is fundamentally launched against Black people, Black forms of life continue to shape what it might mean to be human in deeply profound ways. By this we mean that by reckoning with the multiple violences of antiblackness, Black peoples continually revise what being human means for all of us. The intention here is a quite vast Sylvia Wynter-esque project in which the word resistance is a lazy way to capture the vast dynamics at play. Afro-pessimism requires serious and significant intellectual labor to fully engage its insights. It involves questioning the last 500 years of human existence and seeking the overthrow and destruction of this system.

The work of diversity can often obscure antiblackness and the impenetrable structures that continually produce Black peoples as out of place, as things, and as non-human. Similarly, the turn to POC as a common denominator for non-white people, which Jared Sexton (2010) has called "people-of-color-blindness," is an obscuring gesture too. Sexton points out that POC politics and its insistence on coalition often obscures the specificities of how antiblackness shapes the experiences and realities of Black people's lives. By so doing, POC politics often assumes that one-size-fits-all for addressing issues of racism, especially in the diversity policies of large institutions. Such logics easily reproduce antiblack racism. In the policy context, what often occurs next is that others benefit, but Black folks do not, because Blacks are always structurally located differently in the institutions. The non-white "inclusion" is nonetheless taken as work done to redress questions of racism for all. Indeed, Sexton's intervention is quite evident in the Canadian scene, especially for our purposes today in the academic sector, although one can see this across all sectors of society.

I dedicate this chapter to Andrew Loku's memory. Sitting in my small apartment in a Corman town last summer, I was stunned to hear Kwame McKenzie (Director of Health Equity at Toronto's Centre for Addiction and Mental Health) and Matt Galloway (radio broadcaster with the Canadian Broadcasting Corporation) engage in a conversation that showed more concern for the mental health of the officer who shot Loku than for Loku himself. I immediately used social media to reach out and challenge them, suggesting that police should be disarmed. Galloway responded by saying that disarming was a non-starter. I find such a stance deeply troubling. It points to the ways in which those representing and acting on behalf of power shape the conversations and thusly affect what kinds of political horizons we collectively hold. These two Black men in compensatory individual positions— positions that Black folks are supposed to take as a measure of our inclusion— refused to acknowledge that Black life is always already precarious life.

Similarly, Mark Saunders, Chief of Police of the Toronto Police Services, is meant to mark another moment of Black inclusion. These forms of compensatory individualism are not collective inclusion, but rather anesthetizing projects meant to distract us from the ongoing structural conditions that produce premature deaths for Black people. Using the logics of white capitalist supremacy, compensatory individualism is good value for the status quo but costly for Black people. The total sum is a rough calculation of Black misery and death, with a surplus of whiteness—a cruel mathematics, if you wish.

Possible Turns for Post-60s Studies

The question of resources requires that those of us doing labor under the rubric of Black studies must do more than critique excellently, more than become and train technocrats of the word. We find ourselves in a moment that requires us to articulate a politics for something. What might Black studies or Black Canadian studies be, if it cannot even impact the site of its location and production? As Stuart Hall has reminded us repeatedly, "any politic requires the symbolic drawing of the boundary; there has to be some symbolic divide... No politics is possible without a sense of 'us' and 'them'" (Hall, 1992, p. 8). Post-60s studies in the Canadian academy can begin to engage the symbolic drawing of the boundary through faculty appointments as a start to democratize the institution.

My perspective on these topics and in particular the role of post-60s studies in the university is deeply influenced by Stuart Hall's "Cultural Studies and its Theoretical Legacies" (1992), in which he makes a rather strong case for cultural studies being about something. Hall writes in that essay that cultural studies "is a project that is always open to that which it doesn't yet know, to that which it can't yet name" (p. 263). Hall continues:

> It is a serious enterprise, or project, and that is inscribed in what is sometimes called the 'political' aspect of cultural studies. Not that there's one politics already inscribed in it. But there is something at stake in cultural studies, in a way that I think, and hope, is not exactly true of many other very important intellectual and critical practices.
>
> *(Hall, 1992, p. 263)*

Hall further states: "I don't believe knowledge is closed, but I do believe that politics is impossible without what I have called 'the arbitrary closure'" (p. 264). In so doing, Hall further suggests that cultural studies is not just about any political project but rather about very specific political projects and political projects that change over time. Following Hall, we might inquire about the political projects of our time that post-60s studies might turn its attention to.

In particular, I am interested in Hall's phrasing of an "intellectual practice of politics." This turn of phrase asks that we—the practitioners and audiences of post-60s studies—do something. It does not proscribe what that something is, but asks that when we identify what that something is, that we act in ways that reveal its potentialities for reshaping the world in more just ways. I want to bring this notion of the "intellectual practice of politics" to its most local concern for us here—the site of the university; the academy. We all recognize the university as a site of struggle, and we are all capable of pointing to the many flashpoints of those struggles. I point to one flashpoint among the many as an example of the failure of Canadian post-60s studies to engage in the "intellectual practice of politics" in relations of antiblack racism.

Part 2: Institutionalizing the Fictions of our Collective Politics

It is to the mid-1960s' movements of possible liberation that I direct this chapter. It was the promise of those movements and their potential to produce a different configuration of planetary life that gave us our current languages, from which our political desires now urgently require rescue. Anti-colonial, Indigenous, feminist, gay and lesbian liberation, civil rights and human rights movements and now their siblings—disability, Trans, asexuality and so on—have come to mark the limit case of rethinking planetary life forms. This is to say, the collective struggle against systems of injustice that emerged in the 1960s has unraveled into a series of often competing identities, marking the very limits of what was imagined in that decade.

There are two significant temporal markers that hold the ideas of this chapter together—post-World War II, and post-1989. These two moments produced logics of life and potentialities, or lack thereof, which continue to shape and thus limit our imaginaries. Indeed, in all the cases I listed above, an appeal to human or civil rights is framed by the logics of post-World War II and the UN Declaration of Human Rights as central to their politics and their imaginaries. Similarly, one might understand the collapse of the Berlin Wall in 1989 and the resultant unraveling of state communism as impeding radical imaginaries, producing alternatives to capitalist organization of planetary life. Again, one might argue that the conditions produced by post-war rights discourses and practices, and the interruption of imaginaries in part induced by the fall of the Wall, have now become hegemonic conditions. In such a circumstance, the neoliberal organization of life has rendered most politics reformist. Significantly, the present stalemate is one characterized by rhetorics of inclusion and niche placement that often does not fundamentally question the foundational arrangements that have produced the institutional and structural conditions of contemporary life. And, let us be clear, the logics of reconciliation operate in the same fashion.

Indeed, much of our politics in this moment remains stuck in either policing the borders of the mid-60s' movements or attempting to expand them. This policing and expansion is otherwise known as inclusion. I am against inclusion. It is precisely the ongoing obsession with trying to get it right, and the privileging of those movements as still useful for late modern capitalist life, that limits our potential to think of life otherwise. Drawing on Adolph Reed Jr. (2010) and his analysis of post-desegregation Black politics in the United States, we should understand such stagnation or boundary wars as a form of demobilization. Reed notes that:

> the regime of race relations management as realized through the four-pronged dynamic of incorporation that I have discussed has exerted a demobilizing effect on black politics precisely by virtue of its capacities for delivering benefits and, perhaps more important, for defining what benefits political action can legitimately be used to pursue.
>
> *(Reed, 2010, p. 121)*

In my view, Reed's analysis works across all the mid-1960s' movements. Those movements have been incorporated into the existing logics and structures of late modernist capitalism; reaping benefits for few but producing the assumptive logic that such benefits are extendable to all. Significantly, when we look at such practices in their specificity, what we see most clearly is that the extension of benefits not only demobilizes more radical calls for transformation but also simultaneously produces disposable populations in its wake (the logic I am pinpointing here is that symbolically and actually, my inclusion in the academic community comes at the expense of thousands of Black people rendered uneducable). Such performative gestures, rather than structural destruction, are currently the means whereby late modern capital "devours its most cogent critics with no apparent lack of indigestion," as William Haver (1999, p. 26) once put it. It is precisely for this reason that the value of inclusion requires a rigorous (re)engagement—in the many senses and ways that value might be invoked, especially its monetary and racial logics. Indeed, my argument is premised on the idea that value is always already linked to capital and its racial economy rather than ideas about human work, which I believe have come to be the foundations of diversity, equity, anti-racism, and social justice.

The compensatory individualism that characterizes our present moment requires a rigorous refusal. Falling under the logic of inclusion, but a singular inclusion, we are expected to celebrate individual "success" as if it is collective. By refusing compensatory individuals, we are forced to value differently what is at stake for Black lives in a context that seeks to include only those of us who sit the furthest away from what Wynter (2003) calls the dysselected other—that is, the Black subject. Make no mistake about it, current logics of anti-racism, equity, and even social justice have as their other the Black subject. We never collectively benefit from their institutional performativity. The benefit is reserved for those closer to white—white not only as phenotype, but as instituted antiblackness and thus white supremacist logics.

One might suggest that where the mid-1960s' movements stalled was in their inability to rethink and put into place their own movements, and then beyond, a different and sustainable idea of value that could reside outside of late modern capitalist logics, immune to the seductive pull of inclusion and performative rhetoric of representation of bodies, identities, and community. Lyndon Barrett (1999), writing with the contested theorizations of value, asserted that:

> To interpose no alternative value in the theoretically neutral moment of calling value into question remains equivalent to strengthening and reincarnating reified, dominant value.
>
> *(Barrett, 1999, pp. 52–53)*

That the social movements of the mid-1960s in their broadest sense did not rethink value (or, only at their most radical extreme) means that the promise of a different order of planetary life was immediately compromised. The conditions for incorporation were made possible and therefore manageable in the existent order and structure. The conditions therefore became adaptable to include without substantive change. Again, as a pessimistic aside, let me be clear that the benefits won by those movements are not meaningless. However, we must now come to see those benefits for what they are: won at the expense of deepening an already deadly culture. In some ways, my arguments return to a perverse structural Marxist critique, but with crucial differences that will be elucidated throughout the remainder of this chapter.

The Problem with Value in a Performative Discourse of Excellence

The problem of re-orienting value is an important one for any future that seeks to produce a world in which value exists beyond the orbit of the present financial-ization of life. Thus, my critique of Canadian anti-racism discourse is that it fun-damentally operates from a belief in the sutured narrative of adequate, potential, and possible representivity in the institution. In other words, the foundation of its thought is locked in a performative discourse of excellence and merit; the very terms that makes the idea of anti-racism necessary in the first place. While looking back at the historical invention and necessity of anti-racism, its invocation would be somewhat different from the dominant discourse. However, it adopts the same terms of the system it claims to want to unmake, in order to be intelligible. Indeed, anti-racism as a performative discourse functions to obscure rather than to specify. Sexton (2010) writes:

> We might, finally, name this refusal people-of-color-blindness, a form of colorblindness inherent to the concept of "people of color" to the pre-cise extent that it misunderstands the specificity of antiblackness and pre-sumes or insists upon the monolithic character of victimization under white supremacy – thinking (the afterlife of) slavery as a form of exploitation or colonization or a species of racial oppression among others.
>
> *(Sexton, 2010, p. 48)*

It is precisely for the reasons that Sexton outlines that diversity, equity, anti-racism, and social justice, as terms no longer make sense to me as avenues for Black liberation or any kind of liberation for that matter. Such terms obscure the varied and multiple conditions that have come to frame our livability in profoundly dif-ferent ways. But, importantly, such terms seem to suggest that justice can be had in a structure and system that is only possible as long as injustice is present, given that it is founded in injustice. Therefore, I find myself considering the work that such terms do, who benefits from the performative dynamics of such terms, and how such terms function to deny Black lifeforms a planetary presence beyond late modern capitalism. In my view, it is our responsibility to rethink the terms that now in their faulty execution produce the fictions of our collective politics.

In the present conjuncture such terms seek to rescue failed nation-state prac-tices, especially in the wealthy west, where the stark evidence of violent exclusion remains clearly visible. The languages and practices of diversity, equity, and social justice are state-saving devices, not devices of or for a potential freedom. In this fashion the material and ideological work of such terms work to keep in place the very conditions that they are meant to ameliorate. But more insidiously, such terms work to continually produce hierarchies of the human in terms of how material wealth and the ideas attached to it are distributed to representative members of ethno-political collectivities. In each case when these political settlements are achieved, Black people find themselves at the bottom of the distribution scales. The position that Black people occupy is in indeed in accordance with the ongoing and still world-defining position instituted most forcefully post-1492. These languages, with their attendant ideas continue to replicate an unequal and unjust system. Their proliferation works to produce legitimacy for the network of institutions founded on the degradations of Black unfreedom. Their deployment works to pre-empt deeper desires for change, institutional reformulations, and ultimately freedom.

Thus, what we refer to as diversity, equity, social justice, and anti-racism still too often rely upon the rhetoric of the institution and its structural apparatus as the bias of its critique, as though the institution itself is power and not a performative representation of power at work. Such a critique means to suggest that the intended audience of diversity, equity, social justice, and anti-racism's address can at least be tacitly in alignment with a different but similar foundation for the social as we presently know it. As the opposite side of the same coin, the performative qualities of diversity, equity, anti-racism, and social justice become quickly complicit with stabilizing knowledge and thus commodifying it or being devoured by the institution and the corporation. The department I work in is a case in point: its very name, Social Justice Education, is a serious farce of institutionality that is reliant on the very thing it claims to want to change.

The failures of white liberal feminism and the resulting debates have been some of the most important moments for pushing knowledge claims forward in the context of the post-1960s academy. In the context of these claims, bell hooks' *Talking Back: Thinking Feminist, Thinking Black* (1989) remains a singularly important contribution to many of us who came to age politically in North America in the 1980s. hooks' insights in *Talking Back* included her audacity to speak back, not only to feminism, but to blackness as constitutively male. This opened a critique that allowed many of us to speak publicly of the many concerns that we lived as immediacies, but could find neither the courage to utter it nor a politically engaged language to speak it, even if we were brave enough. Black feminists and other feminists of color, many of them lesbians, opened up an entire terrain of knowledge claims and injunctions to act politically that helped to signal a substantive change in patterns of knowledge production and quite frankly, "what could be asked and argued over." In short, they helped to usher in the "culture wars" and bring the crisis of knowledge to its boiling point in all the disciplines. hooks' essay "on being black at yale: education as a practice of freedom" (1989) remains for me an important manifesto about the North American academy and the ethical responsibility of Black studies and Black scholars.

hooks writes, concerning some Black academics:

> Black academics are not individually confronted daily with the horrendous acts of racist discrimination and exploitation that once served as constant reminders that the struggle to end racist domination could not cease—that our lot remains intimately connected with the fate of all oppressed black people, in the United States and globally. This has led many black scholars to become unmindful of the radical traditions established by black educators who were deeply committed to transforming society, who were not concerned solely with individual progress or simply transforming facts about a particular discipline.
>
> *(hooks, 1989, p. 63)*

What hooks places on the agenda is an ethical imperative to act beyond one's individual interests. The academy's pathological hatred of Black women is something to behold. I don't make this claim to get some kind of feminist or womanist kudos. In my various positions over 20 years in the academy, I have witnessed how colleagues respond to Black women's presence in the academy. In almost every instance that a Black woman is mentioned, there is an attempt to move on to something else, to delegitimize, or to blatantly ignore. This position can only be understood in light of the ways in which Black women's feminist politics have retained the most significant critique of state and institution of any contemporary feminist politics. This insistence is one that consistently uncovers the ruses of diversity and inclusion as ongoing forms of violence, meant to incorporate a few at the expense of the many.

Part 3: A Politics of Thought

So, how might the question of equality be re-posed as a concern that distinguishes itself from what generally passes as anti-racism in the Canadian academy? One essential element is a broad-based engagement with questions of multicultural difference as incommensurable with the foundational doctrines of the university. In this way, equality is not reduced to merely numbers (although we cannot discount numbers) and representative bodies and experiences, in this case always marked as colored. Instead, the struggle over equality becomes one in which the forms of knowledge being produced, disseminated, and actively engaged lead to a constitutively different university.

In this regard it is my argument that what we might call "Black freedom" is in distinct opposition to something called capitalism. Given that the Black body was indeed an instrument of capital, as well as a significant producer of it—that was both commodity and labor—the question of freedom and capital is a particularly knotty one for Black personhood. At the same time, given the intimate crossing of blackness and capitalism, "Black freedom" as an "authentic" possibility inaugurates a challenge of the imagination to produce new modes of living that might be in accord with some of the most radical global "Indigenous" calls for a different kind of world—a world beyond reconciliation gestures and its empty politics. It is precisely in the moment that Black personhood can be accorded its full human status that "new forms of human life" enter the world. If we take seriously that the problem is one of culture rather than "nature" or "history" or even "economics," as Wynter has argued, then the task before us becomes clearer. Wynter (2003) states that we operate from "a specific culturally instituted order of consciousness," (p. 20) and further argues that it is "the phenomena of culture… that provides the ground of all human existential reality or actuality" (p. 21). With such in mind then, Wynter has, across a body of work, suggested that culture is the site of struggle and transformation and that a "new" culture can be instituted. Because I am a Wynterian, it is at this point that I part ways with afro-pessimism.

This returns me to value. Fred Moten (2003) has taken Marx to task in terms of the relation between value, exchange-value, and the commodity. In his reading of Marx, Moten highlights that Marx could not imagine the commodity that shrieks. By that Moten places Frederick Douglass' Aunt Hester's scream as embodying the tension of value and commodity that Marx's thought failed to grapple with. Indeed, this gap in Marx has been one that most Black intellectuals have had to grapple with as they move with and through Marxism, and still hold it as central to some kind of collective possibilities. The invitation to enter these institutions— universities, policing, media, even presidencies—revealed the manner in which contemporary performative acts of inclusion reside in the longer history of Black enslaved life.

Therefore, much like C. L. R. James (1996), I want to suggest that making this case is not about "racial chauvinism" (p. 11) but rather about making clear the ways in which logics of degradation, humiliation, and oppression continue to work. As James points out, "any excessive sensitiveness to black chauvinism by the white revolutionaries is the surest way to create hostilities and suspicion among the black people" (p. 11). The same remains so today, prohibiting our move toward a possible decolonial future. For example, the suspicion with which the Black Lives Matter movement is greeted confirms for many the immovability of the deep structures of antiblack racism, those that the afro-pessimists have argued must be entirely destroyed.

Finally, what I have come to call a pure decolonial project (Walcott, 2014), an adaptation of Jacques Derrida's (2000) "pure hospitality" thus attempts to unmoor the silences that condition our contemporary moment by risking identity in favor of a politics of thought. Pure or purity of the proposed politics marks an open- ing to that which we cannot know in advance of our desires and encounters. By "politics of thought," I signal the ways in which coloniality's most profound operations work at the level of what it means to know and how knowing places some bodies out of place. Knowing, and what it means to know, produce the death worlds bodily and otherwise, including the environmental disasters all around us, which began in the moment of colonization and racial slavery. These death worlds are both historical and urgently present, and through them we might conceive of forms of relationality in which new modes of human-ness might be possible. The demand here then is to think of new possibilities for human life beyond capitalist modernity. In a post-communist world, on a neoliberal globe, our present challenge is to think, articulate, and move toward different and new modes of human life. A pure decolonial project works to produce new modes of relational logics and conditions in which the intimacies that European colonial expansion produced for us might be refashioned. But most importantly, a pure decolonial project arrests and subtends languages that promise to move toward transformative relations of being, but instead are in collusion with that which we already have. To work against institutional disregard of Black life, new imaginaries are necessary and urgently needed, beginning with our language. Indeed, all the necessary code words for desiring to achieve justice are deeply tainted and have come to represent flawed practices in which Black people are repeatedly placed on the lowest rungs at the point of practice and institutionalized enactments. The language, then, of a desired justice requires a constant and shifting revision, a revision that remains steps ahead of our present coloniality. As I suggested earlier in this chapter, the only accomplishment of the long colonial moment transformed into neoliberal coloniality has been its interruption of our imaginations. Imagine anew, yet again, and always.

Works Referenced

Barrett, L. (1999). *Blackness and value: Seeing double.* Cambridge: Cambridge University Press.

Foster, C. (2015, November 9). Canada's blacks: Still waiting for their moment of 'real change'. *The Globe and Mail.* Retrieved from www.theglobeandmail.com/globe-debate/canadas-blacks-still-waiting-for-their-moment-of-real-change/article27175310/

Hall, S. (1992). Cultural studies and its theoretical legacies. In L. Grossberg, C. Nelson & P. Treichler (Eds.), *Cultural studies* (pp. 277–294). New York and London: Routledge.

Haver, W. (1997). *The body of this death: Historicity and sociality in the time of AIDS.* Stanford, CA: Stanford University Press.

Haver, W. (1999). Another university, now: A practical proposal for a new foundation of the university. In K. Armatage (Ed.), *Equity and how to get it: Rescuing graduate studies* (pp. 25–37). Toronto: Inanna Publications and Education Inc.

hooks, b. (1989). On being Black at Yale: Education as a practice of freedom. In hooks, b. (Ed.), *Talking back: Thinking feminist, thinking black* (pp. 62–72). Toronto: Between the Lines.

James, C. L. R., & McLemee, S. (1996). *C. L. R. James on the "Negro question".* Jackson, MS: University Press of Mississippi.

Lee, E., & Cross Cultural Communication Centre. (1985). *Letters to Marcia: A teacher's guide to anti-racist education.* Toronto: Cross Cultural Communication Centre.

McMurtry, R., & Curling, A. (2008). *The review of the roots of youth violence. Volume 1: Findings, analysis and conclusions.* Toronto: ServiceOntario Publications.

Moten, F. (2003). *In the break: The aesthetics of the Black radical tradition.* Minneapolis, MN: University of Minnesota Press.

Nopper, T. (2011). Minority, black and non-black people of color: 'New' color-blind racism and the US Small Business Administration's approach to minority business lending in the post-civil rights era. *Critical Sociology, 37*(5), 651–671.

Reed, A. (2010). *Renewing Black intellectual history: The ideological and material foundations of African American thought.* Boulder, CO: Paradigm.

Sexton, J. (2010). People-of-color-blindness: Notes on the afterlife of slavery. *Social Text, 28*(2), 31–35.

Simpson, L. (2013, November 6). I am not a nation state. *Nations Rising.* Retrieved from http://nationsrising.org/i-am-not-a-nation-state/

The Canadian Press. (2015, November 5). Trudeau's 'because it's 2015' retort draws international attention. *The Globe and Mail.* Retrieved from www.theglobeandmail.com/news/politics/trudeaus-because-its-2015-retort-draws-international-cheers/article27119856/

Walcott, R. (2014). The problem of the human: Black ontologies and "the coloniality of our beings". In S. Broeck & C. Junker (Eds.), *Postcoloniality-decoloniality-Black critique: Joints and fissures* (pp. 93–108). Frankfurt: Campus Verlag.

Wilderson, F. B. (2010). *Red, white & black: Cinema and the structure of U.S. antagonisms.* Durham, NC: Duke University Press.

Wynter, S. (2003). Unsettling the coloniality of being/power/truth/freedom towards the human, after man, its overrepresentation—an argument. *CR: The New Centennial Review, 3*(3), 257–337.

6

WHEN JUSTICE IS A LACKEY

Leigh Patel

I

"Wakanda is in chaos…Villainy rules. Justice is a slave."

Ta-Nehisi Coates, *Black Panther*

So begins the story of T'Challa, the King of Wakanda. Wakanda is in ruins, the kingdom is in danger of never recovering, and T'Challa must resurrect the ethics of the African continent's most accomplished and wizened people. This resurrection is far from a simple task, as the would-be defenders and guards of the nation are themselves in various positions against each other, determining political strategies for survival and compromise, and staving off vulnerability in less-than-ideal ways. While the tale of T'Challa and Wakanda is fictional, the struggles for justice, including determining what can constitute just action amidst so much confusing co-opting of power, echo contemporary pressure points in education and society in compelling ways. Coates' writing casts justice as a figurative and perhaps literal slave to possibly highlight the literal attenuations done to justice so that harm, malfeasance, and profit may more soundly preside over well-being.

I frame this chapter through Coates' introductory words to hold still contexts of justice in education, to think of them through the figurations of enslavement and servitude, so that we might be able to ascertain the ways in which injustice is populating justice. In part, I use the figurative language precisely because the language of justice is so ubiquitous that it's tempting to assume shared literal definitions. What if we revisited the meaning of justice in education in such a way that demanded a reckoning with uses that display more servitude than morality? I propose that this is precisely the place to consider justice in education: in a state of sophisticated servitude, wherein the term has been so thoroughly leeched of meaning that its constant utterances do the work of hierarchy and power.

To engage with the editors' questions of where injustice comes from and what justice in education wants, we have to forcibly hold off the prevailing, widely held tendency to refer to justice as singularly defined and immune from injustice. Considering justice as intertwined with injustice, ironically doing the labor of injustice, opens a space to apprehend this unseemly relationship. This is not to say that justice must always be entangled in injustice but that its current conditions of being invoked from troublesome stances, such as conscious capitalism,[1] require being able to view justice and injustice simultaneously, even mutually constituting each other. From a stance that considers the collocation of justice and injustice, we can view justice not just as an ideal and far-off goal that may be realized in the future, but how its invocation has become servile to a sophisticated project of stratified well-being and safety. Here, sophisticated does not mean stylistics but rather the development of deep complexity, such that simplistic practices, whether created in the name of justice or not, are insufficient in their core conceptualization of reality. Reckoning with a sophisticated project of stratification necessarily renders facile approaches appropriately inutile. To intervene on facile uses of justice, it is necessary to begin with a grounding in the foundational logics and structures that stratify, erase, and spectacularize different populations in distinct ways for a common purpose of domination: coloniality.

Coloniality, which casts some beings as higher and others as lower, seeks to stratify for the purposes of dominion. The project of coloniality, and the creation of race as a construct for the purpose of stratification, has its beginnings as early as the encounters of Europeans in the Americas and Africa. The United States was formed as and maintains a settler colony structure, in which theft of land, erasure of indigeneity, and the attempt to collapse blackness into chattel are ongoing yet incomplete projects. Settler colonialism, as Patrick Wolfe has defined it, is a structure, not an event. Settler migrants invade a land to occupy it, claim it, and turn it into property. The settler structure depends, simultaneously, on the attempt to convert land into property, Indigenous people to disappear, and the creation of chattel labor that both works the land and is property itself (Wolfe, 1999). The occupation of land is never finished, Indigenous people must always be disappearing, and there can never be enough property, land, and chattel, in the hands of a few. Since contact invasion, the structure of settler colonialism has been maintained by eradicating and punishing Indigenous, Black, and Brown peoples. In settler colonialism, as well as other forms of coloniality, well-being and safety are stratified, partitioned, and reserved for some.

The material structures that stratify well-being have developed accompanying narratives to justify and fuel deep inequity such that doubletalk, contradictory standards, and rationales for everyday violence are the facts of life that in turn create social death (Cacho, 2012). The irrationality of obviating humanness from profoundly human experiences is echoed in myriad social spaces and function in complex ways across epistemic and physical geographies, while also operating with specific precision. Consider three examples of this sophisticated irrationality in the field of education:

April 2015

Thirty-five Black American teachers in Atlanta, Georgia, were indicted with criminal charges for falsifying school assessment data. Of those 35, twelve were formally sentenced, with fines ranging from one to five thousand dollars and jail time from one to five years. That same year, nine white teachers in New York were charged with grade changing and test coaching. To date, four have been dismissed from their jobs, and six in total have paid punitive fines, but none has been sentenced with prison time. The teachers in Georgia were charged with prison sentences because their charges included racketeering, a federal crime that is defined as "conspiring to organize to commit crimes, especially on an ongoing basis as part of an organized crime operation" (Fantz, 2015). The judge in the case repeated several times that *all* the teachers were asked to do was admit their guilt and forfeit their right to appeal, and that without that, he would turn to sentences of incarceration. Georgia and New York are among 40 states that have reported widespread falsification of test score results since scores have been attached to teacher pay and job security, school closings, and withholding of funding.

October 2015

A school safety officer in South Carolina was called into a high school class-room to remove a student who had refused to comply with orders from her teacher. In a video that became viral for its graphic racial violence, the white officer threw the 16-year-old Black girl down to the floor, while still at her desk, and then wrenched her away from the desk and tossed her several feet across the classroom floor. The officer was dismissed, and later that same week, about 100 students walked out of school to protest the firing of the officer, using the hashtag #BringBackFields. Spring Valley High School, where the incident occurred and was videotaped, has an enrollment of 50% Black students, 34% white, 8% Hispanic, 7% Asian and other races. The school's demographics have shifted from majority white in 1994 to majority Black in 2014 with 38% of the students eligible for free or reduced lunch. The majority of the students who protested to bring the white officer back into the school and on the state's pay-roll were Black.

April 2016

In a feature-length story, the *New York Times* reported on Georgetown University's sale of 272 enslaved people in 1838, a sale that was organized by two of the Jesuit university's presidents to pay off the institution's debts. The sale was unique for its size but not unique as a palimpsest for the intricate histories of higher education and systemic racism (Wilder, 2014). The newspaper feature highlighted the work of two men, an historian employed by Georgetown and a graduate of the institution who established a non-profit to investigate the details and legacies of the enslaved people. As reported by Rachel Swarns, the historical and genealogical research provided:

> a glimpse of an insular world dominated by priests who required their slaves to attend Mass for the sake of their salvation, but also whipped and sold some of them. The records describe runaways, harsh plantation conditions and the anguish voiced by some Jesuits over their participation in a system of forced servitude.
>
> *(Swarns, 2016, para. 18)*

Justice and injustice are embroiled in all three of these cases. How could an education system that has consistently institutionally monetized and criminalized Black life (Sojoyner, 2013) explicitly consort with a legal system of codified rights to demand guilt and public apology for racketeering in the face of the largest federal policy that explicitly creates winners and losers, profit holders and debtors? How can we make sense of the affinity that some Black youth unsurprisingly developed for a racially abusive white police officer to the extent that their demand for justice was to reinstate this embodied symbol and manifestation of racialized state surveillance (Gilmore, 2007)? How to contend with the racialized emotionality (Ioanide, 2015) of priests, themselves informed by ideals of Ignatian social justice, who attempted to simultaneously own people and break them of their will and shepherd them through spirituality? All speak to a sophistication of racialized systemic violence in which justice has become a servant to injustice. In each of these instances, a mere smattering of the everyday domination and social death that marks modernity, justice is deeply implicated in the momentum of injustice. Justice is not an unfortunate casualty that has been left in the ruins by injustice. Justice and injustice are irrationally breathed in the same case, with justice doing the bidding of injustice.

Societies created to operate under logics of coloniality (Wynter, 2004) have developed sophisticated, complex, invocations of justice that are lackeys to the purposeful injustice of hierarchical creation and sequestering of resources. Justice has become servile to the whims and irrational logic of gendered and racial violence that is deeply needed to differentially confer and deny relative subject positions under the state. In the face of diffuse yet conjoined architectures of profit and safety for some at the expense of others, narratives of justice are needed to blur and obviate the core unjust structure. In this sophisticated version of racist capitalism, materially dismantling intertwined white advantage (Delmont, 2016; Roithmayr, 2004) is screened off by official neoliberal platforms of diversity, inclusion, and individual rights (Melamed, 2011). As a particularly pungent example, outlined thoroughly by

Delmont (2016), the court-ordered racial desegregation of schools in the United States in 1954 was rolled back from its mild directive of all due speed almost as soon as it was passed. The over-determined and media-hyped white backlash in Boston predated desegregation efforts in other cities so that the coverage could stave off those integration efforts nationally. Delmont makes the case that racial integration was blocked by a number of connected, concerted efforts, including the leveraging of rhetorics of safety and rights for the interest of the racially advantaged white population. As one white mother explained to a white television journalist, "These are our civil rights and we're taking advantage of them" (as quoted in Delmont, 2016, p. 25). The narrative of an always already endowed white right to property justified injustice through the very language of rights and justice.

The centuries-long project of settler colonialism and its manifestation of racist capitalism have long relied on a sizable and shapeshifting gap between word and deed (Perry, 2011). This double-switching system is so deeply engrained that debt and profit, guilt and innocence are simultaneously invoked, often in contradictory fashion, but implicitly legible for the overriding purpose of property rights for a few at the expense of many. To bifurcate the appeals of justice as being necessarily protected from the tentacles of injustice, then, is to miss how justice can be and is co-opted constantly. Recent scholarship in the area of critical higher education studies has productively situated appeals for diversity within power structures of heteropatriarchal capitalism. For example, in her examination of the work of diversity offices and personnel on college campuses, Ahmed (2012) offered a sobering picture of how ensnared diversity is in the property logics of image and status. Ahmed depicts, through empirical interviews with diversity workers, that the large part of the work of diversity is to enact representational justice but not transgress those representations.

One imaginative challenge is to understand justice and injustice as intertwined, with justice reflecting the material coordinates and needs of injustice. Another challenge, though, is situating how justice serves injustice within particular fields. While coloniality is consistent in its goal of hierarchical stratification of being, it takes specific shape in distinct yet connected ways. Social fields must consider, then, what are the particular epistemic patterns that predominate in the field that may be seeding hierarchy and stratified well-being, in order to understand how those seedlings feed malignancy in other social fields. Within the field of education, with its popular imaginative place of enabling upward social mobility and altering uneven playing grounds, linearity and progress are particularly important narratives to examine for the ethno-geographies of injustice and justice.

II

It gets better
A step in the right direction
Forward progress

These phrases are metonymies for the widely held narrative and trope of linear progress. Metonymies are figurations that hold strong material force because of the vast references contained within the shorthand reference (Perry, 2011). "The White House" stands for myriad policies and histories of the executive branch of the United States. A "suit" stands in for upper middle-class and elite managerial and ruling classes, often male. Metonymies enact tremendous force because they are widely held quick references that both attempt and fail to contain the various subject locations around the reference. This is, in part, how narratives can obviate societal structure. They seem to stand for shared experiences but actually collapse the nuanced positions within the shared edifice.

Ideas of justice in education, and more broadly, in society, are deeply connected to the metonymies of linearity. Linearity is the governing belief that not only is there a straight line between two points, but that this is the best, and solely valid, line. Other connections between points are lesser, if visible at all. The metonymy of linearity is teleological and normative at once. In its normative force, of winnowing what is better and desired, it presents a knowledge-for project (Wynter, 2004) that overrepresents validated knowledge frames while obscuring the purposes those frames are actually serving. In other words, linearity is overrepresented not because it is objectively true but because asserting it as the truth of progress enacts and protects power. A power that can ensure that suffering from below can be ameliorated through a straight line of progress, a premise that does not bear out statistically, to say the least, is a narrative of linearity, a knowledge project for maintenance of a stratified settler society.

Much of Sylvia Wynter's work to-date has mapped the ways that knowledge-for projects have constituted figurations of science and beingness for the purpose of cordoning off elevation for some and subjugation for others. Within this work, Wynter traces how "science is produced as an objective system of knowledge that enumerates and classifies 'difference'" (McKittrick, 2015, p. 145). It is a knowledge-for project that serves the newly rational, but fundamentally irrational, over-representation of Man that is deeply coupled with the location, the creation, and enclosure of less than Man. Wynter's work has much to bear for any engagement of beingness and justice, but of particular resonance here are her analyses that biocentric versions of the rational man, an outcropping of modernity in the nineteenth century, continue to thrive and obscure the simultaneous ways that culture and consciousness are entangled. They compose the constant knot of being, with how we think influencing our brain, and vice versa. More than a mere assertion of duality of being, Wynter exhaustively demonstrates how the science of modernity has wrongfully bifurcated culture from cognition, leading to profound misunderstandings of how realities are mutually constituted in conceptualization and experience.

To understand justice as entangled with, servant to, injustice is to temporarily draw into focus the woeful failure of progress as only sequential and linear when considered alongside the sophisticated, complex state of coloniality. The entanglement of justice and injustice occurs culturally and neurophysiologically. "A step in the right direction" facilitates material relationships to fundamentally wrong and harmful realities. It suggests first and foremost that a move toward justice must inherently include and mark a move away from injustice. When problematic frames of justice are annotated as a step in the right direction, they are partially innocentized in their incompleteness, and a latent theory of progress as sequential forestalls imagining multiply constituted justice and injustice. This forestalling is how material possibilities are created through cultural practices.

The overriding epistemology of linearity cannot countenance movement outside of binaries of either/or, forward and backward, progress and regression. Grief, for example, is commonly described as having a number of distinct stages. But if one's experience of grief is cyclical, refreshed, remixed, and anything but finished, that experience is outside of the more dominant, linear frame of grief as experienced through stages, with the last stage being acceptance. The ubiquity of linearity literally demarcates how lives are to be lived and grieved. In other words, the epistemology of the straight line can materially shape ontology. The idea that a move toward justice is a move away from injustice is itself a seduction that invites a feeling of ease in the face of so much wrong. What a relief to make a move in the right direction when exponential and deeply intertwined scales of death, suffering, and containment mark the aggregate human experience.

The tropes of linearity are not mere rhetoric. They fuse and short-circuit the divergent, contested, and defiantly lived onto-epistemologies of the foldings-in of justice with injustice. Consider the following portion of a speech given by then U.S. Secretary of Education, Arne Duncan, in 2010:

> Today is a great day! I have looked forward to this day for a long time—and so have America's teachers, parents, students, and school leaders. Today is the day that marks the beginning of the development of a new and much-improved generation of assessments for America's schoolchildren. Today marks the start of Assessments 2.0.[2]

Duncan's reference to 2.0 does more than suggest a progression from a mythic first wave of assessments in schooling; it negates the obvious analysis of high stakes assessments having accelerated, like gasoline to a flame, existing inequities in the structure of schooling. Abundant research has documented the racialized harm that federally mandated and privately sourced scientific assessments have wrought through education (e.g., Mayorga & Picower, 2015). From the explicitly racist frames of science of phrenology to the softer antiblack coding in studies on the lack of grit and perseverance in dispossessed populations of color, assessments have long done the bidding of self-perpetuating rationalizations of a race and class-segmented social order. Duncan's framing of a much-improved generation does not engage with the harms of past generations but pushes forward a linear idea of progress, long awaited by many, if not all. The referent of "generation" invokes this era as younger, descendant, and better. It imprints the settler expansionist narrative of manifest destiny that justifies seizure of land and removal of Indigenous peoples as the necessary progressive project of civilization (Veracini, 2010). The narrative relies on and is articulated through its sole protagonist, the white male explorer who antithetically speaks for all. The picture of assessment given by Duncan all but encloses the ability to analyze the created scientific project of monetized educational assessment as it has conjoined with criminalization, resulting in the knot of injustice that has led to Black teachers being convicted of racketeering. Linear figurations of assessment obstruct education's abilities to contend with the deep irony of how it has consistently activated, delivered, and leveraged antiblack racism and then charged Black teachers with having organized to steal from the institution. Lines, particularly unidirectional lines of progeny, purposefully cannot contend with knotted complexity of irrational logics sustained and morphed for consistent material impacts. A new generation must mean movement away from the older generation's limitations.

Linear tropes of progress and incremental advancement also obscure the collocated reality of inequity and injustice. As a project sourced from colonial logics of property and well-being for some, formal education in the United States has been a consistent location of stratification and intertwined material advantage for those at the top of the strata. Moreover, it has never accomplished this alone, nor has it ever remotely existed outside of the concomitant structures of the law, housing, healthcare, incarceration, family, and the media. Linearity, though, winnows in a focus on a singular field as a focal point for ascertaining the shape of progress. The field of educational research is deeply complicit in conflating test score production for learning (Patel, 2015), but it could never have done this by itself. This conflation relied on media and policy framings of school success and failure, the capital interests in the development of assessment measures for profit, the codification of legal property rights to create and govern assessments, and the resultant income from infringement of codified property rights. Each of these components is differentially located within a unifying structure of whiteness as property (Harris, 1993). Schools have been tied to property and profit since their inception by European settlers (Lomawaima, 1999), and liberal humanist frames of rights and criminality underwrite aggregate discriminatory patterns of incarceration (Murakawa, 2014). Although media frames, legal codes of property rights, and educational policies are researched in distinct disciplines, they operate together in lived unjust realities of domination and subjugation.

When linear narratives focus attention on one line of progress, injustice is able to proliferate more fully through these intertwined structures. Even though the teachers convicted of, in essence, organized crime, were ensnared in the racialized policies of education and law, justice as defined by the law and enacted in the courtroom forestalls this analysis. Sojoyner (2013) brings to bear how even the critical analysis of the school-to-prison pipeline obscured the actual enclosures that schools themselves have become. This is not to say that deep analysis of each social field cannot yield insights into how justice and injustice are taking shape, but that analyses of how injustice has yoked justice for materially harmful purposes is significantly weakened when only one social field is entertained. It is easier to maintain that education assessments can themselves be a sign of progress if analyses of privatized profits and incarceration are sequestered as off-topic. Similarly, the angst of Jesuit priests who were at once charged with materially harming and guiding enslaved Black people to deliverance is rendered more clearly when viewed through the ways that Christianity has, often, furthered the expansionist needs of settler property rights. The material experience has been shaped by the narrative.

Wynter's points again resonate about the collateral damage that hierarchical knowledge-for projects have produced in shaping our lived conceptualizations of ourselves. McKittrick explains:

> Wynter's project thus encourages noticing very specific and meaningful cognitive leaps—that are underwritten by colonial encounters—that uncover the knotted intersections between scientific thought, colonialism, race and racism, cognition, identity, time, and space.
>
> *(McKittrick, 2015, p. 148)*

A contemporary example of these leaps is found in a refraction of analysis of the history and politics of racial segregation in United States schools. In 1979, Derrick Bell put forward an analysis of the Supreme Court Brown v. Board of Education that situated the decision as a compromise to stave off converging credibility crises for the nation. He described the decision as an instance of interest convergence, that rarity of when white material interests loosen somewhat in order to secure the longer term material gain. While many uses of Bell's analysis maintain an examination of instances in which white material advantage is strategically loosened for larger material holding, interest convergence is also used as a strategy for managing diversity and cultural interactions (e.g., Felder & Barker, 2013). These uses of interest convergence present a wholly different interpretation and use than what Bell put forward. While it is the nature of ideas to shift and be shifted, and I do not wish to suggest that meanings can or should be frozen, it is also our responsibility to consider the effects of the reshaping of meanings. Words and meanings are impermanently yoked together, but that yoking is always in context. Questioning the meaning in context can yield insight into how culture and cognition are materially shaping each other and requisite possibilities for life, and perhaps, justice as well. In this case, the original analytic tool of interest convergence has been shifted from its original mapping of racist property rights to a strategy for collating racialized interests. Bell's analysis that interest convergence serves to ultimately reseat white material interests then no longer has a place in the theory when it is refurbished for aims of diversity and institutional approach. It is but one deeply ironic stance, of multiple forms of antiblack violence (Mayorga et al., 2015). Wynter's points about the shape of our practices and how we think of them prompt for analyses of justice in education that contend with how it is being intricately shaped by the longstanding, multi-dimensional project of injustice in education.

When justice is a prisoner in a web of incarceration and foreclosures, it cannot manifest liberation in one single move on a line.

III

> I just found it real ironic how everyone that was around me whom I thought to be very optimistic people were dreading those days, and I always knew I'd be cool. I never felt like this was going to be a rough time for me. I knew that there were going to be rough times for the Earth because of [sic] this system is based in entropy, and it's pretty much headed in a certain direction. It's time we all reach out for something new.
>
> *Prince Rogers Nelson (1999)*

What can be a way for justice when the available ways are bankrupt for ease of life yet drenched for settler fantasies of progress and justice? To go forward in a different way than linear progress, we have to reckon with past and present in a different, complex way.

I return to the ruins of contemporary Wakanda in *The Black Panther* (Coates, Stelfreeze, & Martin, 2016). Wakanda was the most technologically advanced African nation. The history of the nation was of self-determination, strategic visibility, and collective pride. In its recent realities of struggle and schism, members of the elite female guard, the Dora Milaje, struggled to defend a king who has been absent. While their defense of a nation is reconceptualized from a very different history than a settler colony, they return to their past to rethink their future (Dillard, 2008). Lessons lie within.

The United States has an altogether different history and therefore different contemporary existence from which it must imagine its futures than does Wakanda. Disorder and chaos rumble under orderly rhetorics of justice, representation, and rights (Robinson, 2016). As Robinson demonstrates, this disorder is made possible and strengthened because the "relationships between such understanding and social institutions are tautological rather than dialectical" (p. 208). Robinson also suggests that the mythical existence of this tautological loop is ruptured when it is perceived as myth. Narratives facilitate structures. When mythologies of justice, linearity, and progress are apprehended as contingent, the contingencies may be more open to realignment.

The task of rethinking justice is etched in the words of Prince, whose words of entropy and reaching beyond for something new articulate the ethic that imaginative leaps must distance themselves from harmful, malignant narratives. Releasing these fictions and their handmaiden harms can open up new ways of collective that are rendered ineligible and illegible within settler scripts (Tuck, Guess, & Sultan, 2014).

It is, of course, no surprise that Prince did not personally identify with the entropy that he could adroitly conceptualize. Neither is it surprising that this disidentification, a sampling in order to move away from (Muñoz, 1999), was the raw material with which Prince navigated and remade his own contingent relationship with property rights, well-being, and Black futurity. The field of education has some distance to cover if it is to tap into an articulation of justice for the expansion of well-being rather than property. This distance is not along a single line. But if nothing else, we should be able to learn, to undo what we have known to know something altogether new. It will undoubtedly be difficult to imagine ourselves in relation to learning. It will be unsettling, even dangerous, but that core act of learning is the field's just responsibility.

Notes

1 Conscious capitalism is a book, explicit platform of many corporations, and present in many schools of business as a topic of study. It has become a cultural practice in the structure of capitalism.
2 Thank you to Dr. Eve Tuck for suggesting a reading of the speech by Duncan in this analysis.

Works Referenced

Ahmed, S. (2012). *On being included: Racism and diversity in institutional life*. Durham, NC: Duke University Press.

Bell Jr, D. A. (1979). Brown v. Board of Education and the interest-convergence dilemma. *Harvard Law* Review, *93*, 518.

Cacho, L. M. (2012). *Social death: Racialized rightlessness and the criminalization of the unprotected*. New York: NYU Press.

Coates, T. (w), Stelfreeze, B. (p), and Martin, L. (i). *Black Panther* #1 (2016, April). Marvel Comics.

Delmont, M. F. (2016). *Why busing failed: Race, media, and the national resistance to school desegregation*. Oakland, CA: University of California Press.

Dillard, C. B. (2008). When the ground is black, the ground is fertile: Exploring endarkened feminist epistemology and healing methodologies in the spirit. In N. K. Denzin, Y. S. Lincoln, & L. Tuhiwai Smith (Eds.), *Handbook of critical and indigenous methodologies* (pp. 277–292). Los Angeles: Sage.

Duncan, A. (2010, September 2). Beyond the bubble tests: The next generation of assessment—Secretary Arne Duncan's remarks to state leaders at Achieve's American diploma project leadership team meeting. U.S. Department of Education, transcript available: www.cnn.com/2015/04/14/us/georgia-atlanta-public-schools-cheating-scandal-verdicts/

Fantz, A. (2015, April 15). Prison time for some Atlanta school educators in cheating scandal. Retrieved from www.cnn.com/2015/04/14/us/georgia-atlanta-public-schools-cheating-scandal-verdicts/

Felder, P. P., & Barker, M. J. (2013). Extending Bell's concept of interest convergence: A framework for understanding the African American doctoral student experience. *International Journal of Doctoral Studies*, *8*, 1–20.

Gilmore, R. W. (2007). *Golden gulag: Prisons, surplus, crisis, and opposition in globalizing California* (Vol. 21). Berkeley, CA: University of California Press.

Harris, C. I. (1993). Whiteness as property. *Harvard Law Review*, *106*(8), 1707–1791.

Ioanide, P. (2015). *The emotional politics of racism: How feelings trump facts in an era of colorblindness*. Palo Alto, CA: Stanford University Press.

Lomawaima, K. T. (1999). The unnatural history of American Indian education. In K. G. Swisher & J. W. Tippeconnic III (Eds.), *Next steps: Research and practice to advance Indian education* (pp. 2–30). Charleston, SC: ERIC Publications.

Mayorga, E., & Picower, B. (2015). *What's race got to do with it?: How current school reform policy maintains racial and economic inequality*. New York: Peter Lang.

Mayorga, E., Mazid, I., Wun, C., Sojoyner, D., & Bradley, J. (2015). Call for conversations. *Berkeley Review of Education*, *5*(2), 197–218.

McKittrick, K. (2015). Axis, bold as love: On Sylvia Wynter, Jimi Hendrix, and the promise of science. In K. McKittrick (Ed.), *Sylvia Wynter: On being human as praxis* (pp. 142–163). Durham, NC: Duke University Press.

Melamed, J. (2011). *Represent and destroy: Rationalizing violence in the new racial capitalism*. Minneapolis, MN: University of Minnesota Press.

Muñoz, J. E. (1999). *Disidentifications: Queers of color and the performance of politics* (Vol. 2). Minneapolis, MN: University of Minnesota Press

Murakawa, N. (2014). *The first civil right: How liberals built prison America*. Oxford: Oxford University Press.

Nelson, P. R. (1999, December 10). Prince Rogers Nelson's entire 1999 CNN interview. Retrieved from www.cnn.com/videos/entertainment/2016/04/21/prince-rogers -nelson-1999-lkl-entire-interview.cnn

Patel, L. (2015). *Decolonizing educational research: From ownership to answerability*. New York: Routledge.

Perry, I. (2011). *More beautiful and more terrible: The embrace and transcendence of racial inequality in the United States*. New York: New York University Press.

Robinson, C. J. (2016). *The terms of order: Political science and the myth of leadership* (2nd ed.). New York: SUNY Press.

Roithmayr, D. (2004). Locked in segregation. *Virginia Journal of Social Policy & Law*, *12*, 197–259.

Sojoyner, D. M. (2013). Black radicals make for bad citizens: Undoing the myth of the school to prison pipeline. *Berkeley Review of Education*, *4*(2), 241–263.

Swarns, R. (2016, April 16). 272 Slaves were sold to save Georgetown. What does it owe their descendants? *The New York Times*. Retrieved from www.nytimes.com/2016/04/17/us/georgetown-university-search-for-slave-descendants.html

Tuck, E., Guess, A., & Sultan, H. (2014, June 26). Not nowhere: Collaborating on selfsame land. *Decolonization: Indigeneity, Education & Society*. Retrieved from https://decolonization.wordpress.com/2014/06/26/not-nowhere-collaborating-on-selfsame-land/

Veracini, L. (2010). *Settler colonialism*. Basingstoke, UK: Palgrave Macmillan.

Wilder, C. S. (2014). *Ebony and ivy: Race, slavery, and the troubled history of America's universities*. New York: Bloomsbury Publishing USA.

Wynter, S. (2004). Unsettling the coloniality of being/power/truth/freedom: Towards the human, after man, its overrepresentation—An argument. *CR: The New Centennial Review*, *3*(3), 257–337.

7

THE REVOLUTION HAS BEGUN

Christi Belcourt

Based on a keynote lecture by Christi Belcourt
Maamwizing: Indigeneity in the Academy
Conference at Laurentian University, Sudbury, Ontario, Canada
November 19, 2016

I grew up in Métis politics, and have been attending conferences since I was a young girl, perhaps even while I was still in my mother's belly. I have heard the talks; I have heard the hope; I have heard promises for change. I, myself, have been inspired at conferences. Perhaps those were in my naive days, when I did not know what I know now—that is, what is happening to the earth.

A word of warning: this story ends with a revolution. There has been much talk about reconciliation in the last few years. The term "reconciliation" is used in political circles to rebrand the insidiousness of assimilation as government policy. Reconciliation is neither comfortable nor convenient, and for good reason. Reconciliation without land returned and a correction of all that has resulted from the dispossession of Indigenous peoples is not even possible.

Indigenous peoples and our ancestors have endured 400 years of genocide, murder, and dispossession; the theft of our lands; oppression; colonialism; racism; the theft of thousands of children; the division of families and communities; forced assimilation and sterilization; sickening medical experiments; the torture of Indigenous children; and the attempted destruction of our languages. We continue to be murdered. Our children continue to be stolen by the thousands and assimilated into educational systems that are enshrined into Canadian law. We suffer debilitating poverty and must endure the pompous expressions of superiority by the dominant society at every turn.

Sharing and Generosity

All of this has been thrown at us with the intention of wiping us off the earth as recognizable, sovereign, and distinct nations. It is astounding to me that we are even willing to sit down and talk about reconciliation. How peaceful, dignified, and beautiful Indigenous people are, that we have endured all of this, and yet are still willing to share. Sharing and generosity are at the core of our values.

Sharing and generosity are core central tenets of my life. They are tied to love, respect, and compassion. They are tied to justice, and they are threaded throughout this chapter. We Indigenous peoples have generosity built into our DNA. We understand that our lives are only possible because of the generosity of Mother Earth and other living beings. Our traditional spirituality comes from the earth. My people come from Lac Sainte Anne, originally called Manitou Sakhigan, spirit-like. My people, the Michif people of Manitou Sakhigan, are buffalo, moose, and fish people, and we share this with other Indigenous nations.

Before colonialism shattered our communities and dispossessed us from our lands, we relied on the buffalo for almost everything. We recognize the buffalo as a nation. They were 90 million strong, as we were, before their genocide occurred. The buffalo were annihilated because of the Europeans' hatred of Indigenous peoples. We have songs for the buffalo, and buffalo ceremonies. Buffalo hold the doorways in our sacred lodges, and are at the center of our creation stories.

Our lives were lived on the land with the buffalo, in accordance with the rhythms of the earth. We traveled freely, as did they. The buffalo gave us everything, and I am alive today because of them. Sharing and generosity, as I said, are in the DNA of our people. Our entire worldview and existence were based on the concept of living in balance with all of creation. We understood then, as we do now, that there are powerful spirits in everything and we are at the mercy of these spirits. The waters are viewed as the lifeblood of Mother Earth, so highly regarded that certain lakes were considered off limits to everyone except grandmothers harvesting medicines. Our original place-names hold many of the teachings about the land.

Our relationships to the spirits are marked by extreme gratitude, humility, and respect, as are our relationships with the animals, insects, fish, and birds. We know that we are at the bottom of the food chain, not the top. We need everything to survive, and nothing needs us. Our governance structures were based on animals, spirits, and the earth. We know that all human beings are spirits as well—that we are, in fact, all one. The air you breathe is my breath. The water I drink is part of you.

Chief Seattle once said, "Man did not weave the web of life; he is merely a strand in it. Whatever he does to the web, he does to himself. All things share the same breath... the beast, the tree, the man. The air shares its spirit with all life that it supports." We believed then, as we do now, that all healing comes from the earth. Plants not only have healing powers, but they communicate with us. They carry sickness away. They are generous and kind, and never stop giving all life on earth. My great-auntie, my kokum's sister, told me how her mother used a poplar tree and a hair from her brother's head to cure an abscessed tooth. Now, skeptics and Western medicine will say that this isn't possible—but we live in a world with the most amazing, fantastical creatures. We share the earth with the peacock spider and the tree frog, with a plethora of mothers including moose and bear. We share the earth with butterflies who begin as an egg the size of a poppy seed, who grow and break free, and then weave their own cocoons and shed their old skin, emerging with wings. We live on a giant ball of water floating in outer space, circling a giant ball of fire. If all this is possible, then anything is possible.

The Importance of Land

To determine how we arrived at this point, it is crucial to talk about land. Land is often overlooked when in conversations about reconciliation—the return of stolen lands is not on the table, nor is the opportunity for Indigenous nations to set up their own sovereign and autonomous governance structures. I do not believe that Canadian law is superior to our own. The imposition of Canadian law onto our nations is a continued affront to our existence as self-determining peoples. I want Canadians to begin to grapple with this, as uncomfortable as it may be; to reconcile themselves to the hard truth so they can begin to let go of the lands they have claimed as their own.

The government of Canada creates maps that label 0.2% of the Canadian landmass as "Indian Reserves." But the Indian Act states that this land is owned by the Queen and her heirs forever, set aside for "the use of the Indians." Meaning that none of our land is in our control, according to Canadian law. None of it. How likely does it seem that any people would hand over 100% of their ancestral land to another people who have come from somewhere else? No one. Canada represents the largest land heist in the history of the world.

It is not just Canada, of course. We know that it is also North America; it is Australia. The settler colonial land heist extends to wherever the British Empire and other European countries colonized the world in their mad dash for riches and resources. It is crucial to talk about the reasons why we were pushed off our lands— namely, resource extraction. When the Europeans first arrived on Turtle Island, there were power struggles going on between European countries and monarchies. Their rulers needed wealth from colonized countries to fortify their coffers and support armies to protect them from the invasion of other European powers. So there was a massive resource grab as the ships set sail. Their goal was not to settle, so it is not accurate to call them settlers, nor can we call them explorers. They were exploiters involved in a massive quest to accumulate riches for their own countries.

The Travesty of the Treaties

Their greed has created the situation we are in today, with a series of treaties that was never honorable on the part of the colonizers. Transcripts and historical records show that the Europeans never considered Indigenous peoples as equals or respected us as nations. They always considered us inferior. After the Seven Years' War, a British Member of Parliament, speaking about the English and French peoples on Turtle Island, stated, "Here is a contest between two equals, about a country we're both claiming undivided right to." It is clear that the treaties were fraudulent and were entered into with the colonizers' devious intentions, at a time when Indigenous peoples were starving and under duress. I want to talk about the spirit and intent of the idea that we are all treaty people because we know that, as Indigenous peoples, our intent was honorable. The intent of the British, however, was to obtain our lands as resources. And none of that has changed. The spirit and intent of both treaty partners must be examined. The treaties are fraudulent documents that must be amended to include the Indigenous perspective that is currently wholly absent. Amending the treaties will shake the validity of Canada to the core of its foundations.

Indigenous peoples still occupied our lands and were still practicing our ceremonies when the residential schools were put into place. The reserve system was intended as a temporary solution until Indigenous peoples could be assimilated, and therefore cease to exist as nations. The spirit of the earth and of the land that I speak of is central to our understanding of the world and our well-being as Indigenous peoples. Land and resources (although I do not refer to them as resources) are also the central reason for our dispossession and the vast mistreatment that followed, including the abuses of the residential school system. The loss of land and self-determination is what keeps us impoverished to this day, literally being murdered and killing ourselves in a crisis of suicide. Land is the foundation of everything for us, now and into the future.

Indigenous Languages and Education Systems

Since I am writing to an audience of educators and academics, I want to pivot for a moment to the topic of education. You are likely reading this book because you are committed, you are willing, and you are seeking solutions for change. You come to this chapter with a good heart, and I thank you for being brave enough to read some of the things I am writing that might be uncomfortable. Some of you are probably nodding your heads with each sentence, agreeing with everything I am writing. Educators are in a position with a great deal of power to effect change. You literally have the future of this country in your hands, especially if you are teaching children. You, more than anyone, can set a course for the future that will completely turn things around. I am not one to sugarcoat things on a matter of life and death for our people, so I will be frank. The education system is failing Indigenous children. It is failing Indigenous peoples, but not only that—it is failing Canadians on a massive scale, in part because it is killing Indigenous languages.

Canadians are probably aware that linguicide was a central and overt policy of residential schools throughout Canada (Nicholas, 2011). There is no excuse for

Canada to continue to deny First Nations children the right to public education in their mother tongue. Currently, we struggle to set up language houses and have our kids run down highways to be able to fund them. Many will say that there have been improvements in the past 20 years, and while that may be true, the reality is we are simply out of time. We no longer have the luxury of incremental steps. I have yet to see an example of any child emerging from a public school system as a fluent speaker of an Indigenous language. The public school system is taking up space and strangulating our languages, albeit unintentionally, and failing both Indigenous and Canadian children.

The late Wilfred Peltier of Wikwemikong was way ahead of his time. He was a brilliant orator, a traditional knowledge keeper, a thinker, and a mentor. We are lucky to still have some of his writings with us. In his paper "Education for Survival" (1985), he discusses the imbalance of the current educational system, which creates "crippled human beings." He once stated that the educational system is killing our kids in the cradle. What he meant was that the system itself conditions children's minds away from free thinking.

Before they were put into school systems, Indigenous children were taught through observation by elders. The elders would notice the particular gifts or skills of each child. Children would be encouraged by individuals to fully embrace their unique gifts with the intention of being responsible to and contributing to the whole community or society. Children would be in practice with elders, so that they could master these gifts of lifelong learning. To me, this is what Peltier was getting at. The current educational system programs children to be obedient above all from the time they enter the school building to the time they leave. I went to a school with schedules and bells and structures, so I know this to be true. Schools are set up with the all-knowing teacher at the head of the class, implying that the students know nothing.

Peltier also asserted that the system fails children by creating hierarchies, funneling all children through the same set of expectations where those who do not get the highest grades feel inadequate compared to others. Even worse than the feelings of inferiority are the feelings of superiority—those with the higher grades begin to feel they are better than the other students. Through this example, Peltier was gesturing toward the way our entire species has begun to think. Our belief systems have promoted the idea that greed and the accumulation of individual wealth define success.

Consequences

This has turned us into a lopsided and imbalanced species that justifies violence to our planet and to others. Our entire world as we know it today holds up the concepts of individual rights over the collective, over the rights of animals and waters to exist in health and well-being, following the flawed logic that accumulation of individual wealth under capitalism branded as democracy leads to a better life for all. It is this belief system that is destroying our world. The concept of the individual right to take without giving has set the world on the course for destruction.

Everywhere we look, this planet is being covered by garbage and radioactive waste and waters are being polluted, because of this belief system. There are between 16 and 38 nuclear power plants and numerous nuclear uranium sites located around the Great Lakes. In Canada, there are over 1,000 oil spills each year. A pipeline called "Line 5," which has a 50-year lifespan, has been sitting under the Straits of Mackinac for 65 years. Fifteen years after its shelf life expired, millions of liters of oil flow through it each day, with little public outcry.

The Nuclear Waste Management Organization is currently advocating for a plan to bury nuclear waste in the Great Lakes watershed region, just north of Elliot Lake, and few in Canada are up in arms about it. Entire ecosystems, which took millions of years to form and help sustain the planet, can be destroyed in minutes so that a few humans can profit and live in luxury. The government documents cancers, tumors, and deformities in fish and dismiss them as anomalies. Moreover, 90% of all seabirds now have plastic in their guts, and yet human beings are not completely freaked out. The hatching of chicks is forced, and then 50% of them are thrown in the garbage to be crushed simply because they were born males. And only a few people cry out in objection.

There are consequences to this. Our traditions tell us that we are breaking sacred law. There are consequences to our species and all species on the earth. We human beings must change our way of thinking, away from greed, which circles back to what I first wrote about: the central core and antidote to greed itself is giving. As Indigenous peoples, we inherently understand this, and in this understanding lies hope.

We are spirits here, surrounded by spirits everywhere. This planet and this life leave me in utter awe; in a state of constant gratitude to the animals, the earth, and the waters. What we are currently doing to Mother Earth is reprehensible.

The Water Revolution

Reconciliation, then, is not limited to an idea of us all getting along as we destroy this planet together. In my mind, reconciliation must begin with the animals and the waters. It must begin with us as human beings asking for forgiveness and deciding, together, that we will set a new course based on respect and sharing, so that all living beings can be healthy and thrive. We have come to a tipping point where the earth is simply not able to sustain our insatiable greed and belief in individual rights. We must shift our thinking to have responsibility rather than rights. We are all headed for the same path of immense suffering if we do not become activists and take control. We, the people, have the power to change things. And fortunately, we have entered a new era and there has been a recent shift, and this is a new era of water. We are witnessing, around the world, the rise of what is to be a water revolution led by regular people who want nothing more than to have clean water for their children and a clean world for the next generations. We are also witnessing the lengths to which governments will go to protect corporate interest over the health and well-being of the citizens they purport to represent and protect.

In Elsipogtog, the people faced phalanxes of police in tactical gear with dogs, assault rifles, and tear gas when they tried to stop a Texas fracking company from coming into their territory (Lukacs, 2013). In Standing Rock, people armed with nothing but prayer and songs faced the federal and state police of their own country, decked out in military gear with sound cannons. The water protectors sang and prayed to protect the very river that they lived off from the destruction of the pipeline. The people were shot at close range with rubber bullets, sprayed mercilessly with tear gas, and the company was able to continue work on the pipeline a mile off from where this was happening.

To protect the interests of the corporate shareholders, the police are being engaged against us. If they come to poison the waters here, we cannot be mistaken to think that we will not face this kind of terror from the state if we try to protect the waters. This is happening all around the world. We are witnessing mothers trying to stand up for babies and the next generation. We are witnessing the atrocities of crimes committed against the people, supported by technological advances in warfare equipment used against us rather than to protect us. Corporate greed is winning. We the people have been declared enemies of the state, in which the economy is a ruthless king. We are unprotected now and can no longer look to the state to protect our interests. We have to know that this is only going to get worse for our children and grandchildren.

Tree Spirits Leaving Before the Fire

I had a dream that guides me to this day, a dream that makes me wish I did not understand some things. In this dream, there was a fire raging across the hilltop. The fire was reaching new forested areas. The spirits of the trees standing 60 stories tall rose above the trees and began to walk away from the fire. I depicted this in a painting called *Tree Spirits Leaving Before the Fire*. I stood on one side of a river, where there was a large gathering of about a couple hundred people. An old medicine man told us to look across the river, and watch the spirits walk. Then some jeeps and vehicles came rushing in. It was our people wearing camouflage, retreating in battle and about to face death. They were environmental warriors fighting for the earth. Then the old man took his pipe and walked into the bush, and the people began to follow. It was 20 years ago that I had that dream.

Now, more than ever, our children need to know the power of the serpent. They need to know our sacred lodges and our ceremonies. The next generations need to know the powers of the animals and the sun and the moon that exist as our governance. They need to speak our languages, which contain the wisdom of this great mystery that we live in. Our children need to know that *saabe* is not a myth, that the rocks can open up and that the little people carry medicine. Our children need to know the spirits of this earth. They need to understand the spirits of the water, the offerings, the ceremonies that we have to make to them, which even after a lifetime of study can never be mastered. They need to be taught on the land. Our children need to become masters and scholars in the natural laws laid down by Nanabozhoo. Our children need to believe in the mystery and magic that exist all around us. They need to know and believe that thunderbirds are real.

The only education that our children need is from the land. Educators and academics, you can do more than you realize. You must have the courage to disrupt the system, for the sake of our children and our grandchildren. You must have the courage to join with each other to turn the system on its head. You must rebuild so schools cease being institutions, and return to their natural state of bringing children to the land, and providing mentorships so children can develop their gifts and be free thinkers (Peltier, 1985). In this way, children will be able to find the solutions that we are not capable of due to our conditioning through colonization.

So, what we need is a revolution. A revolution of the mind. We need a revolution of our actions, a revolution of language revitalization. And it need not be violent. It can be as gentle as a grandmother deciding to carry a pail of water around, launching a movement, and reinvigorating the ceremonies in our minds toward protecting the water, as Josephine Mandamin has done. We do not need to bring indigeneity into universities; we need to bring our Indigenous selves out onto the lands to rebuild our ways of learning, to keep this earth and water pure and beautiful for 10,000 more years. We need a revolution that will put our lands back in our control and stop the waters from being polluted. Our children need to be fully immersed in our languages and spirituality and ceremonies, not part-time, but full-time.

Now, I wish I didn't know the things I know. I wish I could just kick back and relax. But we are in sacred times. We are in a spiritual battle for this earth. We need a revolution of people who are willing to follow the pipe, and not halfway. The earth and waters and future generations need us. So, I apologize if this was not the advice you thought you would get. I hope that this will be my last writing for an academic conference ever, because from now on I want to spend all my time on the land. How many more conferences are we going to go to? I was raised going to conferences, so I am not criticizing anybody who goes. I understand. But we really need something different now.

The revolution has begun. We need each and every one of you to write and sing and dance and block roads and protest and quilt and love and make babies and organize and do whatever you can. Put 100% of yourself into this work and protecting the waters, because all of us are needed. We are all being called to stand up—it is why we were born in this tumultuous time, why each and every one of us is alive on the planet right now in this messed-up, tumultuous time. So, don't give up, don't give in, and fight for what you believe in.

All good stories end in a revolution. Miigwech.

Works Referenced

Lukacs, M. (2013). New Brunswick fracking protests are the frontline of a democratic fight. *The Guardian*. Retrieved from www.theguardian.com/environment/2013/oct/21/new-brunswick-fracking-protests

Nicholas, A. B. (2011). Linguicide: Submersion education and the killing of languages in Canada. *Briarpatch Magazine*. Retrieved from https://briarpatchmagazine.com/articles/view/linguicide

Peltier, W. (1985). *A wise man speaks*. Quebec: Amerindianization Pedagogical Services, Indian Affairs.

Works Referenced

8

PEDAGOGICAL APPLICATIONS OF *TOWARD WHAT JUSTICE?*

Deanna Del Vecchio, Sam Spady, and Nisha Toomey

Introduction

Addressing justice in our teaching practices is an important corollary to writing about justice. Inspired by the chapter contributors, who each work on unique justice projects, we have created a compilation of activities that extend and expand on the ideas and themes in this volume. These workshops and assignments are aimed at helping educators, activists, and community organizers discuss a variety of justice issues with their communities. In keeping with the concept of incommensurability, these activities do not presume agreement on the definition of justice or the pathway to justice. Rather, we invite readers to theorize about justice, injustice, social justice, and solidarity as though the meaning of every word is still in question. Differing experiences of injustice compel different dreams of justice that may not be in alignment with one another. In addition, multiple forms of social justice will have relevance for education and educational research.

The assignments that follow attend to the vocabulary necessary for addressing the multiplicity of justice, and guide readers in considering the implications of those differences for justice and education. These concepts include antiblackness, settler colonialism, and futurities, in order to situate these activities within contemporary social movements and their associated current events, such as Black Lives Matter, Idle No More, and the call for Boycotts, Divestments, Sanctions by Palestinian Civil Society. Finally, we acknowledge the "quiet" movement of teachers for social justice over the past two decades, which has been comprised of teacher organizations, conferences, and mobilizations across Turtle Island.

These lesson ideas, assignments, and projects were designed with an eye for applicability in multiple educational scenarios. Not limited to the postsecondary classroom context, these activities can also be used to guide discussion and learning in non-formal learning environments such as workshops with community organizations, or workplaces. To reflect that flexibility, we have used different terms interchangeably to refer to the leader of the activity (teacher, instructor, facilitator) and the participant (student, learner, participant). The activities engage a multiple literacies framework, in which the term *text* does not refer strictly to the written word, but rather encompasses a wide range of forms including videos, songs, and other art forms. In this chapter, these are all referred to as *texts*.

These assignments and group activities are organized into five categories: the incommensurability of justice, justice in the media, differing forms of justice, the meaning of collective mourning, and climate justice. As a set, they aim to help readers practice the interrogation of justice in everyday life. For each chapter assignment, we have identified overarching learning objectives, themes, theories, and additional readings:

Learning objectives provide action verbs that teachers/facilitators can use to help guide them to gauge student/participant understanding throughout the lesson. These are designed as overarching goals, and should not limit the lessons.

Theories are meant to help frame lessons aimed at academic/postsecondary settings, to provide educators and learners with the keywords and frameworks that situate the assignment, so they can expand on their research and learning after the assignments are complete.

Themes are aimed at non-formal educational settings. Facilitators working with these assignments in organizations, at the grassroots level, or in workplaces may draw on the themes to learn more about the topics or provide summaries of their workshops.

Additional texts that support and expand on the topics covered are provided for some lessons. These range from news items to website links to academic journals to books to videos.

As a whole, this chapter addresses, through prompts for conversing and writing, how justice might be theorized more robustly and with more specificity, in order to rethink our relationships with, and without, the institutions we inhabit and the culture(s) we participate in.

SECTION 1

WHEN JUSTICE IS INCOMMENSURABLE

Theories: Antiblackness, settler colonialism, border studies, futurities, decolonization
Themes: Migrant justice, Indigenous solidarity, antiblackness, solidarity

Activity 1: Toward What Justice(s)?

Learning Objectives

* Consider the aims that various justice projects are working toward.
* Apply this analysis to the chapters in this book, using a notational device to indicate where the justice projects discussed are headed.

In the introduction to this volume, the editors encourage us to think of justice as an imperative rather than an end, and to think of our projects as answering a call for social justice. With this emphasis on the "toward" in working toward justice, Tuck and Yang suggest an arrow as a notational device to represent what we are working toward.

Consider the arrow as a symbol and reminder of the intentions and aims of justice projects, as a way of indicating the "toward." Practice this notational device by applying it to the chapters in this book:

* Considering the discussions in each chapter, how would you use this notational device to convey the aims that the justice projects described in each chapter are reaching for? What are the imperatives that each justice project demands?
* What justice projects can you imagine, and how would you represent them with this notation?
* Can you think of a better notational device to use for this purpose?

Activity 2: Conflicts and Intersections across Movements

Learning Objectives

* Define the term "incommensurable."
* Define "settler colonialism."
* Compare and contrast differences, overlaps, and intersections in concepts of justice. How is justice viewed for Indigenous peoples, immigrants and refugees, LGBTQ2A, disabled people, and Black people living in settler colonial societies.

Read

Tuck, E., & Yang, K. W. (2012). Decolonization is not a metaphor. *Decolonization: Indigeneity, Education & Society, 1*(1), 1–40.

Introduction

Think about conflicts happening in the world today. Conflict exists because each side believes they are *justified*, or entitled, to a certain kind of justice. Choose a conflict to use as a case study: examples could be any current local or global event, or something simple you have experienced in your own life. Now imagine what justice looks like for each side. Why does justice look different for different people?

This work may be done individually or in pairs. Participants can find their own examples, or use predetermined examples from the course topic or theme. Each person can take a few minutes to note down their side of the problem or conflict; then come together to discuss as a pair or as a whole group.

Discussion Points

• What did justice look like for each side? Was it conflicting, intersecting, or a little of both?
• How does power (over policies, land, peoples, and money) work to influence who gets justice? Is it sometimes easier for the party with more power to attain justice for their side of the problem?

Discussion on "Decolonization is Not a Metaphor"

Explain the terms "settler colonialism" and "incommensurability" using examples of groups who are fighting for different forms of justice.

Let's deepen our discussion of this issue by immersing ourselves in some different texts. (In a large group, or in small teams as a homework assignment, since the texts are different lengths.)

Text 1

Official music video for "Immigrants (We Get The Job Done)" by K'Naan featuring Residente, Riz MC & Snow Tha Product.
Hamilton: An American Musical (2017, June 28). *The Hamilton Mixtape: Immigrants (We Get The Job Done)* [Video file]. Retrieved from www.youtube.com/watch?v=6_35a7sn6ds

Text 2

"Unsettling Canada 150" video.
IdleNoMoreMedia. (2017). *UNsettling Canada 150* [Video file]. Retrieved from www.youtube.com/watch?v=w1ivWASu5d4

Text 3

"The Skin We're In" documentary film.
Officer, C. (Director). (2017). *The skin we're in* [Motion picture]. Canada: Canadian Broadcasting Corporation. Retrieved from www.cbc.ca/firsthand/episodes/the-skin-were-in

Watch one or more of these videos, and then list the conflicts or problems identified there. In small groups, respond to the following questions:

- What injustices are being identified?
- Which groups are identified as causing the problem? (Note: this could, and should, be broad).
- What would "justice" mean for the issues that are identified? What possible solutions are offered or requested?
- What possible solutions can you think of?
- What would it mean for Indigenous peoples to have justice?
- What would it mean for Black peoples to have justice?
- What would it mean for migrants to have justice?
- Can you identify a social movement that works for justice for the groups identified?
- Can you identify at least one other text that connects to the short video you have been assigned? Explain how it complements or contrasts with the text.

Come back as a large group to discuss and to identify the incommensurabilities and intersections between these quests for justice.

Additional Questions for Discussion

- How are these struggles, social movements, and concepts of justice often obscured or elided by settler colonial culture?
- Does the fact that these struggles are different mean they can't be fought together?
- What are examples of ways and situations in which people are working together to fight injustices?
- How do groups representing Indigenous, Black, and migrant peoples explain or address incommensurability? Find examples on websites, mission statements, etc.
- Thinking into the future, are there ways you would change your thinking about justice in your world? Are there changes to be made for your own practice of and outlook on justice?
- This workshop focused on Black, Indigenous, and migrant peoples living in settler colonial societies. What other groups or movements are missing in this discussion? What does justice look like for them?

Additional Texts

Alcaraz-Ochoa, R., Gutierrez, J., Pelaez, A., & Alemu, D. (2016, July 12). 9 critical points on anti-blackness, immigration and why non-black Latinxs must shut it down too: Open letter to the immigrant rights movement. [Blog post]

Medium. Retrieved from https://medium.com/@Latinxs_in_solidarity/open-letter-to-the-immigrant-rights-movement-re-anti-blackness-and-why-non-black-latinxs-must-shut-ac0baccb6bf2

Dunbar-Ortiz, R. (2014). "Introduction" and "Indian Country" in *An Indigenous people's history of the United States*. New York: Beacon Press. Retrieved from https://nycstandswithstandingrock.files.wordpress.com/2016/10/dunbar-ortiz-2014.pdf

Mingus, M. (2011, February 12). Changing the framework: Disability Justice. [Blog post]. *Leaving Evidence*. Retrieved from https://leavingevidence.wordpress.com/2011/02/12/changing-the-framework-disability-justice/

Miranda, F. M. (2015, December 2). Antiblackness and undoing the territory of migrant justice. [Blog post]. *Decolonization, Indigeneity, Education & Society*. Retrieved from https://decolonization.wordpress.com/2015/12/02/antiblackness-and-undoing-the-territory-of-migrant-justice/

Robinson, C. J. (1983). *Black Marxism: The making of the Black radical tradition*. Chapel Hill, NC: University of North Carolina Press.

Activity 3: Social Movements across Turtle Island

Learning Objectives

- Define the term "social movement."
- Write summaries of the mission/visions/goals of at least three major social movements today.
- Identify key differences and similarities between notions of justice found across varying groups and communities.

Introduction

What does the term "social movement" mean to you? Research this term and compare your own impressions with those of others.

Research

Choose a current social movement and research its associated supporting organizations and activist groups. You may alternately choose to examine the work of one or more prominent activist figures within these movements, or choose two or three justice movements to compare, rather than taking up the work of one group in depth. Examples across Turtle Island include:

- Idle No More
- Black Lives Matter
- Not 1 More

- Justicia for Migrant Workers
- No One Is Illegal
- Boycotts, Divestments, Sanctions by Palestinian Civil Society
- Stand with Standing Rock
- Critical Resistance
- Mining Injustice Solidarity Network
- … or choose any other any group or movement that has been doing sustained work in the name of justice.

Research the movement of your choice by reading up on the group's mission, vision, and list of demands. Search for them in news articles (aim to find at least three), and check out their events via their website or social media. As you research, take note of their notions of justice. These may also be embedded into actions, statements, or the chosen representatives/figureheads who are prominent within these movements. Explore the following questions:

- How are notions of justice taken up by these groups/movements?
- How might notions of justice presented by this group be interrogated by competing or alternate understandings of justice?
- How do the epistemologies of these groups and movements use justice in a way that may be incommensurate with the notions of justice found in other groups?
- How do the concepts used by these organizations and/or movements employ notions of antiblackness, settler colonialism, and futurities, if at all?
- Describe the ways in which the group's messaging and actions specifically employ notions of justice.

You may select to map out concepts of justice in point form, or write a reflective response to what the concept of justice taken up by this group means to you personally. Does this group advocate on behalf of a community you are part of? Do you have lived experiences with this movement you would like to share? Are your own interests, or the interests of your community, incommensurate with the movement you chose? If so, what can be done about this?

Come back as a group and discuss your findings in detail. Have you found groups that are collaborating and working together despite incommensurability? Discuss possibilities for the future that are presented by these collaborations.

Additional Texts

Black Lives Matter. (2016). Black Lives Matter stands in solidarity with water protectors at Standing Rock. Retrieved from http://blacklivesmatter.com/solidarity-with-standing-rock/

Black Solidarity with Palestine. (n.d.). Retrieved from www.blackforpalestine.com

Davis, A. (2016). *Freedom is a constant struggle: Ferguson, Palestine, and the foundations of a movement.* Chicago, IL: Haymarket Books.

Latty, S., Scribe, M., Peters, A., & Morgan, A. (2016). Not enough human: At the scenes of indigenous and black dispossession. *Journal of the Critical Ethnic Studies Association, 2*(2), 129–158.

Walia, H. (2012, January 1). Decolonizing together: Moving beyond a politics of solidarity toward a practice of decolonization. *Briarpatch Magazine.* Retrieved from https://briarpatchmagazine.com/articles/view/decolonizing-together

Activity 4: (in)Justices in the Academy

Learning Objectives

*   Identify and describe specific ways in which academic institutions have worked with or contrary to current moves for justice.
*   Identify ways in which students are working to resist their institutions' complacency—or complicity—around justice issues.

This reflective activity may center on one anchor text, on current events happening on your campus or elsewhere, or on personal experience.

Perhaps as you are reading this, you are a student attending university; or, you are someone who has chosen to leave academia. What does justice look like in academic institutions? Name some examples of where the work of the academy supports or hinders justice movements. How might the academy uphold many of the problems social movements attempt to disrupt?

Are social justice movements working within, without, or against the academy—or perhaps a combination of all three? Explore this question using your personal experience, or through texts, blog posts, or articles that have emerged from your school community.

Discuss what the academy can or should learn or take up from the teachings of movements that work for justice. Are these movements actively working from within, or without the academy? How can these movements rupture widely held belief systems within academia? How does the academy uphold many of the issues these movements attempt to disrupt?

Additional Texts

Moskowitz, P. (2017, February 13). The campus free speech battle you're not seeing. *Jezebel.* Retrieved from http://jezebel.com/the-campus-free-speech-battle-youre-not-seeing-1791631293

Smith, A. (2007). Social-justice activism in the academic industrial complex. *Journal of Feminist Studies in Religion, 23*(2), 140–145.

Winsa, P. (2017, January 15). He says freedom, they say hate. The pronoun fight is back. *Toronto Star*. Retrieved from www.thestar.com/news/insight/2017/01/15/he-says-freedom-they-say-hate-the-pronoun-fight-is-back.html

Activity 5: Juxtaposing Moments of (in)Justice

Learning Objectives

- Analyze historical texts and moments using contrapuntal reading (Said, 1993).
- Identify the treaties or other practices of land theft used to settle the area you're currently teaching in.
- Look to other moments in time to understand how justice can be done and undone at the same time.

This reading activity uses contrapuntal reading, as described by Edward Said (1993), and also draws from Tupper's (2014) method of teaching treaties and settler colonialism to preservice teachers and high school students in Saskatchewan, Canada. Tupper has students examine the treaties that were signed in her region of Saskatchewan, Canada, and then has them compare this to the Indian Act of 1876.

Option 1

Teaching Treaty

Use the treaties/land proclamations that were signed in your region. If there were none (i.e. the land is still unceded), use the Treaty that Tupper uses in her article (2014).
Have students answer the following questions:

- What was promised in the Treaty?
- How does the Treaty view the relationship between the Canadian state and Indigenous people?
- Are there accounts of what Indigenous people understood the Treaty to mean? Is this different than the written account in English?
- What was the context and conditions when this was signed?

Then have students examine the Indian Act (1876), which was passed at the same time as many treaties in Canada and answer the following questions:

- What is different about the way the Indian Act views the relationship between the Canadian state and Indigenous people?
- How can the ideas, promises, and concepts used in the Treaty take place under the regulations and limits of the Indian Act. What is made possible, and what is made impossible?
- What can pairing these two documents help us to understand?

Option 2

Using Tupper's method we can adapt this activity to thinking about justice more broadly. What moments in history have similar versions of this pattern; attempting to achieve justice or fairness on the one hand, and state legislation to recuperate or resecure white supremacy on the other?

Examples

- The creation of Jim Crow in response to the abolition of slavery, and/or following the civil rights era the creation of *The New Jim Crow* (Alexander, 2012); see also *The 13th* (2016).
- The Residential Schools Truth and Reconciliation Commission taking place at the same time as the creation of the much criticized First Nations Transparency Act (2013), see also Palmater (n.d.).

Reading two texts or historical moments side by side, we can see how what was taking place at one moment was complicated or undone by another moment.

What other documents/historical moments could we pair to learn more about a particular moment where justice is sought, and the backlash endured after? What can looking at these simultaneous events in the same moment teach us about what justice was sought, what might have ended up being recuperated by the state, or about how victory and backlash can take place together?

Additional Texts

Alexander, M. (2012). *The new Jim Crow: Mass incarceration in the age of colorblindness.* New York: The New Press.

DuVernay, A. (Director). (2016). *The 13th.* [Documentary]. United States, Kandoo Films.

Palmater, P. (n.d.). Myth of the crooked indians: C-27 first nations financial transparency act. Retrieved from www.pampalmater.com/myth-of-the-crooked-indians-c-27-first-nations-financial-transparency-act/

Said, E. W. (1993). *Culture and imperialism.* London: Vintage.

Tupper, J. (2014). The possibilities for reconciliation through difficult dialogues: Treaty education as peacebuilding. *Curriculum Inquiry, 44*(4), 469–488.

SECTION 2

JUSTICE IN THE MEDIA

Theories: Afro-pessimism, critical race theory, futurity, American studies, media studies, Indigenous theories, land-based pedagogy, refusal, decolonization

Themes: Indigenous rights, nation-states, decolonization, popular culture, community organizing, social media, music, settler colonialism, white supremacy, antiblackness

Activity 1: Social Justice Playlists

Learning Objectives

- Curate music and artistic media to represent specific meanings of justice.
- Examine the role of the music industry in expressing or suppressing notions of justice.

Option 1

Curate your own social justice playlists, individually or in groups. Describe why you chose each song, and the version of justice the artist describes. Find (or create!) a work of art that you would use as your album cover. Design a booklet that would go with your playlist. To do so, answer the following:

- Who is this music being created for?
- What did we learn from this music?
- What is special about it?
- How do the songs in the playlist envision different ideas of justice?
- What specific lyrics best describe justice movements, actions, or moments?
- Are there places where lyrics or verses contradict others within the same song? What does that mean to you?
- Do the songs in your list represent competing forms of justice, or could they take place together?
- Mass media as an industry can exploit and harm artists. Are there situations where these artists seem to have been co-opted by popular culture? Explain.

Option 2

Have students listen to a playlist, album, or song and do a personal response assignment to it, using the prompts above. Have them suggest another song/album that could either speak back to the artist's version of justice, or compliment the version of justice it is expressing.

Examples

- The Coup
- A Tribe Called Red
- Narcy
- Tall Paul
- Kendrick Lamar
- Beyonce – Lemonade

- Dead Prez
- Princess Nokia
- Savage Family
- Chief
- Supaman
- Leanne Betasamosake Simpson
- Chance the
  Rapper – Coloring Book
- Propaghandi
- Public Enemy
- Frank Waln
- Solange – A Seat at the Table

- Frank Ocean
- Lido Pimienta
- Akawui Riquelme
- Drezus
- M.I.A
- The Refugee All-Stars of
  Sierra Leone
- Bob Marley
- Talib Kweli
- Tupac
- N.W.A.

Additional Text

Mays, K. T. (2015). Can we live – and be modern?: Decolonization, indigenous modernity, and hip hop. https://decolonization.wordpress.com/2015/03/12/can-we-live-and-be-modern-decolonization-indigenous-modernity-and-hip-hop/

Activity 2: The Power (or Limit) of the Media to Disrupt Injustice

Learning Objectives

- Examine the limitations and possibilities of the media to promote justice.
- Compare and contrast viral YouTube videos to identify differing forms of justice.
- Explore how media can perpetuate or disrupt popular notions of Empire and race.

In this age of social media, both groups and individuals use YouTube to share their ideas about justice. This activity sends you on a mini-tour of select videos and "media moments" that directly confront, and work to generate different ways of thinking about, justice.

Introduction

What are the two most recent "viral moments" you can think of that occurred on social media? Were these about justice? If so, what agendas of justice did they promote? Can you think of any they obscured?

Research

Pick a media moment below, and find the video or the associated content online. Watch the video, and then read about this situation if you need more context. Address the following questions and tasks:

- What form(s) of justice were the characters in this video asking for? Or, what injustice happened in this media moment to provoke a major outcry?
- What is the overall message?
- Who is this message is aimed at?
- Who (if anyone) is centered in this media? Who (if anyone) is obscured or elided? Why might this be problematic? Or, do you think this was necessary for the overall goal of the message?
- What strategy or strategies are being used to send the message (humor, shaming, criticism, etc.)... do you think this strategy is helpful? Why or why not?
- Is this content asking for change on an individual level, on the systemic level, or both?
- Describe what the media is asking individuals to do.
- Discuss what systemic change needs to happen in order for this to not have to exist.
- This media may be crafted in direct opposition to other current media trends. Describe what those are and why they might be problematic. How does mass media work to uphold or retrench injustices?
- Make a list of themes that are addressed in this media content.
- Find a text that is associated with or connected to this content. Discuss whether it offers critique or support to the content.

Suggested Media

- "Barbie Savior" Instagram account

Barbiesavior. (2017, February 23). Many of you might not know.... Retrieved from www.instagram.com/p/BQ3P_MJlp6E/

- "Africa For Norway" YouTube channel

SAIH Norway. (2012, November 16). *Africa for Norway – New charity single out now!* Retrieved from www.youtube.com/watch?v=oJLqyuxm96k

- Lily Singh's "A geography class for racist people" video

IISuperwomanII. (2017, June 18). *A geography class for racist people.* Retrieved from www.youtube.com/watch?v=8WfEkXvGQhY

- "Yolocaust" campaign

Gunter, J. (2017, January 20). 'Yolocaust': How should you behave at a Holocaust memorial? *BBC News.* Retrieved from www.bbc.com/news/world-europe-38675835
Shapira, S. (2017). *Yolocaust.* Retrieved from https://yolocaust.de/

- Australia Day

Big Sam the Video Man. (2017, January 12). *2017 Australian Inclusive Lamb advert – 'Australia Day'?* Retrieved from www.youtube.com/watch?v=z1oJXIN-AgA
Junkee. (2017, January 24). *Change Australia Day to May 8, Maaaaate.* Retrieved from www.youtube.com/watch?v=tV57_pRGToU

- Reaction to the Kendall Jenner Pepsi advertisement

McNeal, S. (2017, April 5). Here are the best tweets about that Pepsi ad starring Kendall Jenner. *Buzzfeed.com.* Retrieved from www.buzzfeed.com/stephaniemcneal/pepsi-ad-memes?utm_term=.aq7e83PkXx#.njQDE7J943
RollBizTV. (2017, April 4). *Pepsi ad commercial with Kendall Jenner.* Retrieved from www.buzzfeed.com/stephaniemcneal/pepsi-ad-memes?utm_term=.dn687P-Doo#.oeLwo0Pgg

- Hollywood whitewashing

LastWeekTonight. (2016, February 23). *Whitewashing: Last Week Tonight with John Oliver (HBO).* Retrieved from www.youtube.com/watch?v= XebG4TO_xss&list=LLleBDkataNl2Xgb5yLwu9hQ

Additional Texts

Berlatsky, N. (2014, January 17). *12 Years a Slave:* Yet another Oscar-nominated 'White Savior' story. *The Atlantic.* Retrieved from www.theatlantic.com/entertainment/archive/2014/01/-em-12-years-a-slave-em-yet-another-oscar-nominated-white-savior-story/283142/
Cole, T. (2012, March 21). The White-Savior industrial complex. *The Atlantic.* Retrieved from www.theatlantic.com/international/archive/2012/03/the-white-savior-industrial-complex/254843/

Feminista Jones. (2013, July 17). Is Twitter the underground railroad of activism? *Salon.com.* Retrieved from www.salon.com/2013/07/17/how_twitter_fuels_black_activism/

Hartman, S. (1997). *Scenes of subjection: Terror, slavery, and self-making in Nineteenth century America.* Oxford: Oxford University Press.

Gay, R. (2017, July 25). I don't want to watch slavery fan fiction. *The New York Times.* Retrieved from www.nytimes.com/2017/07/25/opinion/hbo-confederate-slavery-civil-war.html

Activity 3: Antiblackness in the Media

Learning Objectives

* Discuss the relationship between racial justice and antiblackness.
* Understand how antiblackness is reinforced through news media and visual images.

Activity

Without a larger view toward Black freedom, racial justice is yet another site for antiblackness. Considering antiblackness as "the condition of Black children's lives," scan popular media for images of and reporting on suffering. How do these images reinforce antiblackness and the limited framework of racial justice? Conversely, how might these images and stories be reframed to embrace anger and mourning as ways of knowing?

Additional Texts

Howard, T. (2013, March). How does it feel to be a problem? Black male students, schools, and learning in enhancing the knowledge base to disrupt deficit frameworks. *Review of Research in Education, 37,* 54–86.

Smith, M. (2016, July 12). Philando Castile's last night: Tacos and laughs, then a drive. *The New York Times.* Retrieved from www.nytimes.com/2016/07/13/us/philando-castile-minnesota-police-shooting.html

SECTION 3

FORMS OF JUSTICE

Theories: Decolonization, refusal in research, Linearity, humanism, metonymies
Themes: Decolonization, community organizing, Liberalism, educational research

Activity 1: Decolonization and Refusal

Learning Objectives

- In your own words, define "decolonization."
- Cite examples of what decolonization means for Indigenous communities.

In her call for co-resistance movements as a way to build a relationship between the Black radical tradition and critical Indigenous studies, Sandy Grande suggests working through a framework of refusal, focusing on knowledge as a means to eradicate oppression rather than a path toward personal gain. She outlines the commitments that would underpin this project: collectivity, reciprocity, and mutuality. Grande sees one manifestation of this as a collective of scholars who work under a *nom de guerre* to "write in refusal of essentialist and identitarian politics, of individualist inducements, of capitalist imperatives, and other productivist logics of accumulation" (Grande, this volume). Dream up a name for such a collective, and write a manifesto to frame and guide their work.

Additional Texts

Simpson, A. (2007). On ethnographic refusal: Indigeneity, 'voice' and colonial citizenship. *Junctures: The Journal for Thematic Dialogue, 9*, 67–80.

Tailfeathers, E. A. (2016). A conversation with Helen Haig-Brown, Lisa Jackson, and Elle-Máijá Apiniskim Tailfeathers, with some thoughts to frame the conversation. *Biography, 39*(3), 277–306.

Tuck, E., & Yang, K. W. (2014). R-words: Refusing research. In D. Paris & M. T. Winn (Eds.), *Humanizing research: Decolonizing qualitative inquiry with youth and communities* (pp. 223–248). Thousand Oaks, CA: Sage Publications.

Tuck, E., Guess, A., & Sultan, H. (2014, June 26). Not nowhere: Collaborating on selfsame land. *Decolonization: Indigeneity, Education & Society.*

Activity 2: Representing Linearity

Learning Objectives

- Define the term "linearity."
- Discuss how the belief in linearity affects various struggles for justice.

Read "When Justice is a Lackey," Chapter 6 in this volume.

In this chapter, Leigh Patel problematizes the assumption that a linear path is the only acceptable path, through critiquing popular phrases:

"It gets better"

"A step in the right direction"

"Forward progress"

As Patel explains, these phrases are metonymies of linearity; examples of "the widely held narrative and trope of linearity" (Patel, this volume), in which moves toward justice are assumed to be moves away from injustice.

In pairs or individually, research to find another slogan or phrase (from political, public service, or promotional campaigns) and discuss how it functions as a metonymy of linearity.

Additional Text

McKittrick, K. (2015). Axis, bold as love: On Sylvia Wynter, Jimi Hendrix, and the promise of science. In K. McKittrick (Ed.), *Sylvia Wynter: On being human as praxis* (pp. 142–163). Durham, NC: Duke University Press.

Activity 3: Prison Abolition and Fugitive Justice

Learning Objectives

- Define "fugitive pedagogy."
- Identify the mission/visions/goals of at least three prison solidarity movements.

Conduct a mini research project on a prison solidarity movement. Possibilities include the Prisoner Correspondence Project, The Ordinary People Society, The Free Alabama Movement, prisonjustice.ca, Joint Effort, the Stark Raven Media Collective, and the Vancouver Prison Justice Day Committee.

- How do these organizations articulate justice for prisoners?
- How are these organizations articulating the "fugitive pedagogy"?
- What links can be made between centering prisoner justice with some other liberation and justice projects described in this book?
- Explain in your own words how these movements understand justice.

Additional Texts

Davis, A. (2016). *Freedom is a constant struggle: Ferguson, Palestine, and the foundations of a movement*. Chicago, IL: Haymarket Books.

Latty, S., Scribe, M., Peters, A., & Morgan, A. (2016). Not enough human: At the scenes of indigenous and black dispossession. *Journal of the Critical Ethnic Studies Association*, 2(2), 129-158.

SECTION 4

THE MEANINGS OF COLLECTIVE MOURNING

Theories: Transnational feminism; Black feminist epistemologies; mournability, biopolitics
Themes: Colonialism, capitalism

Activity 1: Mourning and Capitalism

Learning Objectives

* Identify historical or contemporary moments that represent Indigenous resistance to colonialism.
* Explore the modes of thinking that influence and shape people's relationship to land.
* Define "mournability."

Research a current or historic example of moments where relationships between peoples and their lands become fraught because of colonialism and/or shifting global contexts of extractive capitalism. Examples could include:

* Indigenous struggles across Turtle Island against industries that wish to develop on and/or steal land
* Education systems of tribal peoples across the Indian subcontinent turning from land-based educational practices to ones informed by anglicized/ Eurocentric belief systems
* Residential schools in Canada
* Migrant workers' struggles and abuses across the world
* The development of "special economic zones" across Southeast Asia, taking people from land-based labor into factories, onto fields, and into wage-labor contexts

Find at least three texts that discuss these issues, focusing on the perspectives of those affected.

How can thinking about different forms of relations help us to move away from the modes of thinking that posit violent and fraught relationships between lands and peoples as inevitable?

Note the way that historical occurrences continue to affect the present, and how the present has been informed by past practices.

Within these complex scenarios, write a reflection paper that explores how we can understand—and begin to rethink—violence through Black feminist thought, Third World Feminism, and the concept of "mournability."

Activity 2: Collective Mourning and Commemoration

Learning Objectives

- Research days of acknowledgement, both state and community-based.
- Discuss ways that collective mourning can be a path to justice, and ways it can be co-opted.

Look to moments of collective mourning, or the desire to have collective mourning, that can articulate these relationships and interrupt taken-for-granted understandings of everyday violence.

Make a list of historical moments that are collectively mourned. Consider ones that are given formal state recognition, i.e., statutory holidays like: Remembrance Day, Martin Luther King Jr. Day, and Memorial Day. Consider others that are marked informally by communities or groups, for example, the Trans Day of Remembrance; the SlutWalk; the National Day of Awareness for Missing and Murdered Indigenous Women.

How are these days of mourning and commemoration mobilized? Though many of these days came from activist struggle to officially recognize important people, struggles, and formally mourn, can you list the ways in which these days can be co-opted, or neutralized of their political impact?

How might these moments of mourning pave a path toward more just relations?

Additional Text

Singh, B. K. (2016). Unjust attachments: mourning as antagonism in Gauri Gill's "1984." *Journal of the Critical Ethnic Studies Association, 2*(2), 104–128.

Activity 3: Zine Project: Representation and Mournability

Learning Objectives

- Identify places within the mainstream media where state violence and antiblackness occur.
- Compare and contrast justice within gay rights discourse and justice within trans★ and queer youth of color discourse. Identify similarities, differences, and overlaps, and explain how justice is different or the same for these groups.
- Identify examples of ways or moments in which trans★ and queer youth of color have resisted or struggled against mainstream media's representation of gay rights.

Research and collect the mentions of trans★ and queer youth of color in the global media for the past week. Analyze these stories to find occurrences of violence, oppressions, resistance, and subversion. What role does justice play in these stories?

Identify mainstream (white, gay, cisgendered, middle-class) discourses in these stories. How do trans★ and queer youth of color contrast with these discourses? How do their actions fight back against state violence and antiblackness in the mainstream?

Using headlines, cut out pictures and any other creative content, make a 5–10 page zine that contours and describes the creative subversions of trans★ and queer youth of color.

Additional Texts

Nast, H., & McIntyre, M. (2011). Bionecropolis: Marx, surplus populations, and the spatial dialectics of reproduction and "race." *Antipode, 43*(3), 1465–1488.

Sharpe, C. (2016). *In the wake: On blackness and being.* Durham, NC: Duke University Press.

Singh, B. K. (2016). Unjust attachments: Mourning as antagonism in Gauri Gill's "1984." *Journal of the Critical Ethnic Studies Association, 2*(2), 104–128.

Findings of the Truth and Reconciliation Commission of Canada report. Retrieved from www.trc.ca/websites/trcinstitution/index.php?p=890

SECTION 5

CLIMATE, LAND, AND WATER

Theories: Critical place inquiry, Indigenous theory, land-based pedagogy, Queer theory, 2-spirit identities, trans★/queer erasure

Themes: Climate justice, neoliberalism, social media/networking, school bullying, antiblackness, state violence

Activity 1: White Environmentalism

Learning Objectives

* Identify places within the mainstream media where state violence and antiblackness occur.
* Compare and contrast justice within gay rights discourse and justice within trans★ and queer youth of color discourse. Identify similarities, differences, and overlaps, and explain how justice is different or the same for these groups.
* Identify examples of ways or moments in which trans★ and queer youth of color have resisted or struggled against mainstream media's representation of gay rights.

Read the following articles

Klein, N. (2014, December 12). Why #BlackLivesMatter should transform the climate debate. *The Nation.* Retrieved from www.thenation.com/article/what-does-blacklivesmatter-have-do-climate-change/

Purdy, J. (2015, August 13). Environmentalism's racist history. *The New Yorker*. Retrieved from www.newyorker.com/news/news-desk/environmentalisms-racist-history

Smith Dahmen, N., Elias, T., Morrison, D., & Morrison, D. (2017, January 4). The overwhelming whiteness of US environmentalism is hobbling the fight against climate change. *Quartz*. Retrieved from https://qz.com/877447/the-overwhelming-whiteness-of-the-us-environmentalist-movement-is-hobbling-the-fight-against-climate-change/

Watch the following videos

Text 1

"Angry Inuk" documentary film.

Arnaquq-Baril, A. (Director). (2016). *Angry Inuk* [Motion picture]. Canada: National Film Board.

Text 2

"Cowspiracy" documentary film.

Anderson, K., & Kuhn, K. (Directors). (2014). *Cowspiracy: The Sustainability Secret* [Motion picture]. USA: A.U.M. Films & First Spark Media.

Text 3

"Greening the Ghetto" TED talk.

Carter, M. (2006, February). *Greening the ghetto* [Video file]. Retrieved from www.ted.com/talks/majora_carter_s_tale_of_urban_renewal

Discuss and reflect on recurrent themes in each of these texts. How is the concept of justice represented in the broad issues covered here?

Define and discuss the term *environmental racism*. Research other examples of ways that environmental racism manifests in the world? This could be a theme touched on in one of the texts above, or another case you are aware of. How do settler colonial logics, and the logics of white superiority, manifest in environmental movements?

What is the relationship between migration and the environment? Using examples from the texts, or your own researched examples, identify ways that environmental impacts force people around the world to leave their homes.

Additional Texts

Martell, A., & Blair, E. (2016, September 26). We were forced to work at Western-run mine, say migrants who fled Eritrea. *Reuters Investigates*. Retrieved from www.reuters.com/investigates/special-report/eritrea-mining-nevsun/

McVeigh, K. (2017, May 24). World is plundering Africa's wealth of 'billions of dollars a year.' *The Guardian*. Retrieved from www.theguardian.com/global-development/2017/may/24/world-is-plundering-africa-wealth-billions-of-dollars-a-year

Shiva, V. (1997). Western science and the destruction of local knowledge. In M. Rahnema & V. Bawtree (Eds.), *The post-development reader* (pp. 161–167). London: Zed Books.

Activity 2: Environmental Priorities

Learning Objectives

- Identify large environmental organizations and describe their mandate.
- Critically analyze messaging used by large, mainstream environmental organizations to identify settler colonial logics.

Research a large, mainstream climate justice organization of your choice.

Interrogate all the ways their messaging and actions employ notions of justice, yet might (or might not) follow a neoliberal agenda, or frame and continue to fit within an outlook on human–nature relations rooted in settler colonial logics.

Identify these logics and all the simple and complex ways they are used, for example from:

- Website design
- Language in the mission and vision statements
- Staff member demographics
- Celebrity ambassadors
- The way they process donations
- Other observations

In what ways are questions of Indigenous peoples and relations to land taken up by these organizations?

Contact the organization with a question you craft that relates to human–nature relationships.

Or, find an organization or group conducting a project similar to the one described in this book (the Indigenous youth theatre group). Document why it is that this group's work successfully challenges typical frameworks, and write them a letter to tell them your thoughts. Or, you may find that a group is performing what they think is a challenge, yet is still following a neoliberal logic. Explain this clearly in a correspondence you may wish to send to them.

Additional Texts

Democracy Now. (2015, April 7). Cowspiracy: As California faces drought, film links14 meat industry to water scarcity & climate change. Retrieved from www.democracynow.org/2015/4/7/cowspiracy_as_california_faces_drought_film

Tuck, E., & McKenzie, M. (2015). *Place in research: Theory, methodology, and methods.* New York: Routledge.

Activity 3: Indigenous Resistance, Land Defense, and Water Protection

Learning Objectives

- Define "contingent collaborations" (Tuck & Yang, 2012).
- Identify current land defense actions; understand the context and historical conditions that have created the need to defend land.
- Compare land defense to mainstream environmental politics.

In this activity, read two articles first, then watch a short film together.

Text 1

Dhillon, J., & Estes, N. (2016, December 22). Standing Rock, #NoDAPL, and Mni Wiconi. *Hot Spots, Cultural Anthropology* website. Retrieved from https://culanth.org/fieldsights/1010-standing-rock-nodapl-and-mni-wiconi

Text 2

Spice, A. (2016, 22 December). Interrupting industrial and academic extraction on native land *Hot Spots, Cultural Anthropology* website. Retrieved from https://culanth.org/fieldsights/1021-interrupting-industrial-and-academic-extraction-on-native-land

Text 3

Embree, Z. (2014, July 18). *Healing Walk 2014.* Retrieved from www.youtube.com/watch?v=rUMSQKGKzEA

Option 1: Group Discussion

- What are these struggles about? Where are they taking place?
- How are Indigenous land defenders and water protectors offering a different way to think about environmental activism and politics?
- How might "contingent collaborations" (Tuck & Yang, 2012) be used to support these struggles?

Option 2: Written Assignment

- Research three Indigenous movements to stop pipelines, oil extraction/refining, or protect waterways. (Examples include Aamjiwnaang Water Gathering,

Standing Rock Oceti Sakowin Camp, Unis'tot'en Camp, Chippewas of the Thames Against Line 9).

- Answer the following questions about these movements:
  - Where are they taking place? What are these struggles about?
  - How are Indigenous land defenders and water protectors offering a different way to think about environmental activism and politics?
  - How might "contingent collaborations" (Tuck & Yang, 2012) be used to support these struggles?

Additional Texts

Dhillon, J., & Estes, N. (2016, December 22). Standing Rock, #NoDAPL, and Mni Wiconi. *Hot Spots, Cultural Anthropology* website. Retrieved from https://culanth.org/fieldsights/1010-standing-rock-nodapl-and-mni-wiconi

Moussa, A. (2016, May 13). Women of Palestine and Turtle Island: A land and water issue. *Red Rising Magazine*. Retrieved from http://redrisingmagazine.ca/women-of-palestine-and-turtle-island-a-land-and-water-issue/

NYC Stands With Standing Rock. (2016). Standing Rock Syllabus. Retrieved from https://nycstandswithstandingrock.wordpress.com/standingrocksyllabus/

Simpson, L. (2016). Indigenous resurgence and co-resistance. *Journal of the Critical Ethnic Studies Association, 2*(2), 19–34.

Staff. (2017, February 28). Report suggesting mercury still leaking near Grassy Narrows 'deeply concerning,' chief says. *CBC News*. Retrieved from www.cbc.ca/news/politics/grassy-narrows-old-mercury-report-1.4001775

Standing Rock Syllabus. (2016, November 3). Standing Rock Syllabus NYC Teach In. Retrieved from https://nycstandswithstandingrock.wordpress.com/2016/11/03/watch-standing-rock-syllabus-nyc-teach-in-on-youtube/

CONTRIBUTORS

Christi Belcourt is a Michif (Métis) visual artist with a deep respect for mother earth, the traditions and the knowledge of her people. In addition to her paintings she is also known as a community-based artist, environmentalist, and advocate for the lands, waters and Indigenous peoples. She is currently a lead organizer for the Onaman Collective, which focuses on resurgence of language and land-based practices. She is also the lead coordinator for Walking With Our Sisters, a community-driven project that honors murdered or missing Indigenous women. Her work *Giniigaaniimenaaning* (Looking Ahead) commemorates residential school survivors, their families, and communities to mark the Prime Minister's historic Apology in 2008 and is installed at Centre Block on Parliament Hill commissioned by the government of Canada. She was named the Aboriginal Arts Laureate by the Ontario Arts Council in 2015. In 2016 she won a Governor General's Innovation Award and was named the winner of the 2016 Premier's Awards in the Arts. She is author of *Medicines to Help Us* (Gabriel Dumont Institute, 2007) and *Beadwork* (Ningwakwe Learning Press, 2010). Christi's work is found within the permanent collections of the National Gallery of Canada; the Art Gallery of Ontario; Gabriel Dumont Institute; the Indian and Inuit Art Collection, Parliament Hill; the Thunder Bay Art Gallery, and Canadian Museum of Civilization, First People's Hall.

Deanna Del Vecchio is a PhD student in Social Justice Education at the University of Toronto's Ontario Institute for Studies in Education. Her research uses participatory photography methodology to explore young people's relationships to place, drawing on Indigenous theorizations of place, refusal, and resistance. Her postgraduate work involved a community arts project with newcomer youth that focused on photography and creative writing as tools for self-expression. Deanna's career in education has included classroom teaching from primary to postsecondary, community-based learning, outdoor education, teacher training, and sitting on the Culture, Communication and Information committee of the Canadian Commission for UNESCO. She holds a Master's degree in Art Education from Concordia University in Montreal, and an undergraduate degree in Geography and Biology from the University of British Columbia.

Michael J. Dumas is Assistant Professor in the Graduate School of Education and the Department of African American Studies at the University of California, Berkeley. His research sits at the intersection(s) of the cultural politics of Black education, the cultural-political economy of urban education, and the futurity of Black childhood(s). His recent publications have appeared in such journals as *Harvard Educational Review, Teachers College Record, Race, Ethnicity and Education,* and *Educational Policy.*

Nirmala Erevelles is Professor of Social and Cultural Studies in Education at the University of Alabama. Her teaching and research interests lie in the areas of disability studies, critical race theory, transnational feminism, sociology of education, and postcolonial studies. Erevelles argues that disability, as a central critical analytic, can have transformative potential in addressing issues as varied as inclusive schooling, critical/radical pedagogies/curricula, HIV/AIDS education, facilitated communication, school violence, multicultural education, and the sex curriculum. Her insistence on an intersectional analysis foregrounds the dialectical relationship between disability and the other constructs of difference, namely race, class, gender, and sexuality and its brutal implications for (disabled) students in U.S. public schools and (disabled) citizens in transnational contexts. Erevelles has published articles in the following journals: the *American Educational Research Journal, Educational Theory, Studies in Education and Philosophy,* the *Journal of Curriculum Studies, Teachers College Record, Disability & Society, Disability Studies Quarterly,* the *Journal of Literary and Cultural Disability Studies, Punishment and Society,* and *African American Review* among others. Her book, *Disability and Difference in Global Contexts: Towards a Transformative Body Politic,* was published by Palgrave in November 2012. She is currently working on a book-length manuscript tentatively entitled *Cripping Empire: Theorizing Intersectionality as if Black/Brown/Disabled Lives Matter.*

Sandy Grande is a Professor of Education as well as the Director of the Center for the Comparative Study of Race and Ethnicity (CCSRE) at Connecticut College. Her research interfaces critical Indigenous theories with the concerns of education. Her highly acclaimed book, *Red Pedagogy: Native American Social and Political Thought,* was published in a 10th anniversary edition (2015). She has also published several book chapters and articles including: "Accumulation of the Primitive: The Limits of Liberalism and the Politics of Occupy Wall Street," *The Journal of Settler Colonial Studies;* "Confessions of a Fulltime Indian," *The Journal of Curriculum and*

Pedagogy; "American Indian Geographies of Identity and Power: At the Crossroads of Indigena and Mestizaje," *Harvard Educational Review*; and, "Red-ding the Word and the World," in Paulo Freire's *Intellectual Roots: Toward Historicity in Praxis*. In addition to her scholarly work, she has provided eldercare for her parents for over ten years and remains the primary caretaker for her 89-year-old father.

Crystal T. Laura (PhD.) is Associate Professor of Educational Leadership at Chicago State University (CSU). Crystal's teaching, research, and service have focused on the social foundations of education, diversity, and equity in schools, and building the capacity of school leaders at all levels of the educational trajectory to promote social justice. Crystal began her career as an African-American History and Communication teacher at St. Leonard's Adult High School for formerly imprisoned men and women, and as a personal essayist who wrote to better understand and disentangle the intersections of education and incarceration. Crystal's scholarship on the "school-to-prison pipeline" is informed by her dissertation project, for which she won an Outstanding Dissertation Award from the Qualitative Research Special Interest Group of the American Educational Research Association (AERA), and has appeared in such peer-reviewed journals as *Race, Ethnicity and Education*; *Cultural Studies – Critical Methodologies*; *Gender and Education*; *Critical Questions in Education*; and also in her award-winning book, *Being Bad: My Baby Brother and the School-to-Prison Pipeline* (Teachers College Press, 2014). Crystal is the recipient of the 2016 CSU Faculty Excellence Award in Research, the university's highest honor for distinguished research, along with early tenure and promotion. She lectures across the United States and is a frequent presenter at the annual meeting of the AERA, to which she has belonged since 2006, and currently serves as Chair of the Equity and Inclusion Council.

Leigh Patel is an interdisciplinary researcher and writer who focuses on the ways that narratives facilitate structures. With a background in sociology, she attends to the stratifying roles that schooling performs in society and the constant potential education holds for social transformation. She is Professor of Education at the Graduate School of Education at the University of California, Riverside.

Sam Spady is a PhD candidate in Social Justice Education at the Ontario Institute for Studies in Education, University of Toronto. Her research focuses on the tar sands in Northern Alberta. Talking to people employed in the oil extraction projects in this region, her project traces how labor in this industry shapes critical learning and relationships to land. She grew up in Fort McMurray, Alberta, on Treaty 8 territory and now lives and organizes in Toronto, the Three Fires Confederacy, Haudenosaunee, and Huron-Wyandot territories.

Nisha Toomey is a PhD student in Social Justice Education at the University of Toronto, a Professor in the Department of Social Work at George Brown College, and a member of No One Is Illegal – Toronto. She has been working on migrant justice issues as an educator and community organizer for over a decade. She spent years working alongside refugees on the Thailand-Myanmar border, first with formal education projects, and later with non-formal training programs that worked to create or find safe and decent employment for undocumented youth. Her PhD work explores the nexus of mobility and migration in the modern world: forced travel for safety vs. travel for work or a better life vs. travel for tourism or "humanitarianism." Nisha is always dreaming up creative ways to teach about gender, race, and class hegemony, settler colonialism, and media literacy. The rest of the time, you can find her either thinking about being in the forest, or actually in the forest.

Eve Tuck is Associate Professor of Critical Race and Indigenous Studies at the Ontario Institute for Studies in Education (OISE), University of Toronto. She is a William T. Grant Scholar (2015–2020) and was a Ford Foundation Postdoctoral Fellow in 2011. Tuck's writing and research is on urban education and Indigenous studies. As a whole, her work focuses on how Indigenous social thought can be engaged to create more fair and just social policy, more meaningful social movements, and when that doesn't work, robust approaches to decolonization. Tuck is the author of two recent books, *Urban Youth and School Pushout* (Routledge, 2012) and *Place in Research* (co-written with Marcia McKenzie, Routledge, 2015). She has also co-edited two books, including *Youth Resistance Research and Theories of Change* (co-edited with K. Wayne Yang, Routledge, 2014), and *Land Education* (co-edited with Kate McCoy and Marcia McKenzie, Routledge, 2016). Tuck is the co-editor of *Critical Ethnic Studies*, a new journal published by University of Minnesota Press. Tuck was recognized in 2014 with an early career award from the Committee on Scholars of Color in Education of the American Educational Research Association. She is the co-creator of the Citation Practices Challenge, an effort to be more intentional about our citation practices, to more fully consider the politics of citation. Tuck is Unangax̂ and is an enrolled member of the Aleut Community of St. Paul Island, Alaska.

Rinaldo Walcott is an Associate Professor and Director of the Women and Gender Studies Institute at the University of Toronto. Rinaldo is the author of *Black Like Who: Writing Black Canada* (Insomniac Press, 1997 with a second revised edition in 2003); he is also the editor of *Rude: Contemporary Black Canadian Cultural Criticism* (Insomniac, 2000). Rinaldo is also the co-editor with Roy Moodley of *Counselling Across and Beyond Cultures: Exploring the Work of Clemment Vontress in Clinical Practice* (University of Toronto Press, 2010). His most recent book is *Queer Returns: Essays on Multiculturalism, Diaspora and Black Studies* (Insomniac Press, 2016). *Black Diaspora Faggotry: Frames Readings Limits* and *The Long Emancipation: Moving Toward (Black) Freedom: An Essay* are under contract to Duke University Press. Rinaldo's research is centered in Black diaspora politics, gender and sexuality, and decolonial politics.

K. Wayne Yang is an Associate Professor in Ethnic Studies at the University of California, San Diego. His work transgresses the line between scholarship and community, as evidenced by his involvement in urban education and community organizing. He was the co-founder of the Avenues Project, a non-profit youth development organization, and also the co-founder of East Oakland Community High School. He also worked in school system reform as part of Oakland Unified School District's Office of School Reform. An accomplished educator, Dr. Yang has taught at high school level in Oakland, California for over 15 years and received the Academic Senate Distinguished Teaching Award in 2010. His research focuses on the role of youth popular culture and pedagogy in the emergence of social movements.

INDEX